BENJAMIN BRITTEN

CE

COMPLETE FOLKSONG ARRANGEMENTS

61 Songs

Edited by Richard Walters

BOOSEY & HAWKES

DISTRIBUTED BY

HAL•LEONARD®
CORPORATION

7777 W. BLUEMOUND RD. P.O. BOX 13819 MILWAUKEE, WI 53213

www.boosey.com
www.halleonard.com

CONTENTS

ALPHABETICAL SONG INDEX

Benjamin Britten, drawing by
Kenneth Green, 1944. The artist designed
the original production of *Peter Grimes*.
Used by permission.

PREFACE

Singers of varying descriptions, be they professionals or students just beginning study, can be grateful that Benjamin Britten (1913-76), the greatest twentieth-century composer of opera and vocal music and master of any instrumental forms he chose to tackle, wrote so many folksong arrangements for voice and piano. One would like to think that the serviceable aim of collecting the arrangements together in one affordable volume would have appealed to the composer.

This edition presents 61 songs from eight previously published small sets and collections, many of which have never before been available in transposed keys. The original publications, with dates of release indicated (all Boosey & Hawkes, except as noted) are: *Volume 1: British Isles* (1943); *Volume 2: France* (1946); *Volume 3: British Isles* (1948); *Volume 4: Moore's Irish Melodies* (1960); *Volume 5: British Isles* (1961); *Volume 6: England* (1961); *Eight Folksong Arrangements* (1980, Faber Music); *Tom Bowling and Other Song Arrangements* (2001). Transcriptions for voice and piano of the arrangements for voice and guitar in *Volume 6* have been newly created for this edition. The original publications used the two word form "folk song." Subsequent editions used "folksong." The latter was chosen for this collection. Some of the songs are not actually uncredited folk material, but they were perceived by Britten to be in the same spirit.

After the first set proved to be successful and useful recital repertoire for Peter Pears as singer and Britten as accompanist, the momentum was clearly established for more arrangements to follow, and follow they did, regularly for many years. But why did Britten begin writing folksong arrangements initially? As is often the case with small compositions, there are almost no documented revelations about them from the composer. We must, by necessity, rely on conjecture.

Britten's first folksong arrangements for voice and piano date from 1941, an unsettling year for the composer as well as for the world at large. He and his friend Peter Pears had been in North America since the summer of 1939, first in Canada for a few weeks, then in the United States, primarily on Long Island, New York. Though stimulated and intrigued by the new surroundings, throughout most of his time in the U.S. Britten was in personal conflict about whether he should remain or return to an England at war. This was despite American musical opportunities and performances, the support of his publisher, Boosey & Hawkes, the warmth of welcoming new friends, and the presence of Pears. The indecision wore on him, and he was often ill.

In the last months in the U.S., before he and Pears boarded a Swedish cargo ship in March of 1942 to cross the Atlantic, Britten suffered from depression and a creative block. He later said of the autumn of 1941 and winter of 1942, "My recollection of that time was of complete incapacity to work."[1] Interestingly, the very first folksong arrangements, comprising most of what would become *Volume 1: British Isles*, come from this period, composed sometime before recitals with Pears in Grand Rapids, Michigan, and on Long Island in November and December, 1941. These songs are "The Salley Gardens," "Little Sir William," "The Bonny Earl o' Moray," "Oliver Cromwell" and "The Ash Grove."

In his letters of 1940 and 1941 Britten raised the subject of homesickness repeatedly. In the spring of 1940 he wrote to a British friend, "You see—I'm gradually realizing that I'm English—& as a composer I suppose I feel I want more definite roots than other people."[2] And in a letter from June, 1941, the composer wrote, "I am homesick, & really only enjoy scenery that reminds me of England."[3] In the summer of 1941 when in California, Britten and Pears discovered an article by E.M. Forster, "George Crabbe: the Poet and the Man," describing not only the poet from Britten's native region of Suffolk, but also vivid descriptions of the Suffolk coast. It made a deep impression on the composer. This famously and eventually led to the creation of *Peter Grimes*, drawn from a character in Crabbe. But in that year, at the time, it contributed greatly to his longing for Britain. Whether consciously or not, this stirring up of an internal homeland in his heart and mind must have contributed to the decision in the autumn of 1941 to set British folksongs for voice and piano.

In an essay written by Britten for the January/February 1941 issue of the American magazine *Modern Music*, "England and the Folk-Art Problem," there is plenty of evidence that he had been contemplating folksong. The "problem" of the title is a discussion of why nationalistic music deliberately based in folksong (distinctly different from folksong arranging), as was championed in Britain by Parry, Grainger, Vaughan Williams and others, was not possible in Britten's viewpoint. The aesthetic issues of a former age are difficult to fully recreate today, but Britten must have felt the need, when turning to folksong arrangements, to avoid the sentiment of previous British composers in the genre. He made some interesting and paradoxical observations in the article. "The chief attractions of English folksongs are the sweetness of the melodies, the close connection between words and music, and the quiet, uneventful charm of the atmosphere. This needfulness however is part of the weakness of the tunes, which seldom have any striking rhythms or memorable melodic features. Like much of the English countryside, they creep into the affections rather than take them by storm." [4] Despite any misgivings, he found them worthy of his attention.

Of course, Britten did not just arrange English folksongs. Scottish, Irish, Welsh, French and Appalachian songs figure in his arrangements, even one German folksong. This makes sense considering his international outlook and his experience in sometimes setting languages other than English in his song cycles and works for voice and orchestra.

Were the 1941 first folksong arrangements partly an attempt to conjure a sense of home? Did the childhood memory of his late mother singing folksongs, to which he sometimes made reference, have anything to do with the idea? Did the modesty of the musical task appeal to him in a period of low creative energy? There probably are no answers to these and the many other possible speculative questions about the genesis of the folksong arrangements.

The decades-long recital combination of Peter Pears and Benjamin Britten was just beginning to establish itself when in North America. Though Britten had written the sublime *Seven Sonnets of Michelangelo* for Pears in 1940 in the U.S., they had not yet publicly performed the cycle. There was a need for repertoire if they were to perform any music by Britten on the 1941 recitals of November and December. Were the folksong arrangements then purely purposeful? Did the idea for them start with Britten or with Pears?

Britten was an extremely practical composer, his practicality informed greatly by his role as performer. He stated throughout his life that the artist should serve the community, including unsophisticated audiences outside the cultural capitals. In his 1964 speech upon receiving the first Aspen Award, Britten stated, "I believe in occasional music. Almost every piece I have ever written has been composed with a certain occasion in mind, and usually for definite performers. When I am asked to compose a work, I want to know in some detail the conditions of the place where it will be performed, the size and acoustics…the kind of people who will hear it, and what language they will understand." [5] It is likely that the folksong arrangements, written to be performed in small cities and towns in the U.S. and in England after their return, were that theory in action.

There is another clue in Britten's public words that might apply directly to the topic. In a 1946 broadcast on BBC, Britten stated, "That is another way for a young composer to keep himself alive, by writing the kind of pieces that a publisher likes to have—pieces that are not too difficult to understand and easy enough to perform." [6] Was this among his thoughts in 1941 as he composed his first folksong arrangements?

In arranging folksongs Britten's aim was a creative one, responding to songs freely, as a composer responds to literary and musical stimulus. He did not go out into the field and collect folk tunes in the way of some composers of various nationalities of the late nineteenth and early twentieth centuries. Such musical study of culture, and the nationalistic implications of it, was outside of his interests. He was content primarily to use published collections as his sources.

Though occasionally the folksong arrangements were written for other singers, they were overwhelmingly conceived for Pears and Britten to perform together in recitals. *Volume 6: England*, for Pears to sing with guitar, is the exception. It may have been that the songs of this set, arranged in 1956, were a warm-up in composing for the guitar in the 1957 cycle *Songs from the Chinese*.

Why Britten chose any of the specific songs to arrange, and obviously rejected countless others, is part of the mystery of why any music is written and where it comes from. For any given song, was it the shape of the melody, its singerly nature, the way the words lay on the notes and rhythms, the harmonic possibilities? Was it its story, its stated or unstated point of view, its poetry or artlessness, its drama or lack of drama, its comedy? Did some of the songs hold personal nostalgia for Britten? Sometimes a particularly vivid character portrayed in song probably interested Britten, a musical dramatist and opera composer. The combinations of tunes and words simply must have appealed to him, for whatever reasons, and sparked his imagination. An entire book could be written analyzing Britten's folksong arrangements, their specific relationships to the rest of his work, and the musical and psychological reasons for arranging each of the folksongs. Perhaps at times it was as simple as Pears or others suggesting folksongs for arranging. Maybe it is best to raise the issues and encourage those who spend significant time teaching, learning, practicing and performing the songs to come up with their own well-earned thoughts about what caused Britten to choose a song.

Britten's selection of song is interesting to consider, but his treatment is even more intriguing. Try this experiment. Cover the piano part completely and learn just the vocal line of a Britten folksong arrangement, forming your own thoughts about what the song is about, its character and subtext, and how it should be sung. Then add Britten's piano accompaniment. You'll see what a strongly individual interpretation he brought to it, likely forcing you to consider musical and interpretive alternatives that had not previously occurred to you. This simple exercise can be an instructive lesson in the basic question of any conscientious and insightful performer: what did the composer—or arranger—intend?

By 1959 Britten had composed 47 song arrangements for voice and piano, had orchestrated 22 of them, and written an additional six for voice and guitar. Though Britten and Pears continued to perform them into the 1970s, Britten wrote no more folksong arrangements for voice and piano after 1959. Perhaps he simply felt that they had plenty of this repertoire. Or perhaps he lost interest in arranging folksongs. His return to it in 1976 was out of necessity. No longer able to accompany Pears on piano, due to illness that affected the use of his right hand, he arranged *Eight Folksongs* for voice and harp for Pears to perform without him. Again, as ever, Britten was a practical composer. The notion of writing new material for Pears to perform with another pianist was obviously avoided.

The word "arrangement" seems almost an insult to Britten's creations, or to any of the major composers interested in such treatments (Bartók, Copland, Mahler, Brahms, and many others). Though the harmonic palate is more limited than in his art songs, these are fully considered, complete compositions built around an existing melody. They are art song treatments of folksongs. The ideas for the arrangements probably formed quickly in his head. All of Britten's compositional values are found in each of them: leanness, clarity, restraint, satisfying structure and phrase, expressiveness without sentimentality, a sure sense of harmony and form, lyricism, wit, and the finishing of every detail. Each piece is a tight, organic composition, usually based on one or two simple motives, sometimes exploring the use of canon. Any young composer could learn from the efficiency of the arrangements; they are among Britten's most transparent works. A sense of playfulness and the pleasure of the task are apparent in the arrangements, qualities found in the work of all great composers.

In describing his composition teacher Frank Bridge's influence, Britten made remarks that ring true in studying all his work, including the folksong arrangements: "In everything he did for me, there were perhaps above all two cardinal principles. One was that you should try to find yourself and be true to what you found. The other—obviously connected with it—was his scrupulous attention to good technique, the business of saying clearly what was in one's mind. He gave me a sense of technical ambition."[7]

An interesting footnote about folksong arrangements involves Britten's longtime friend Aaron Copland. When Copland wrote his first set of arrangements for voice and piano, *Old American Songs*, Pears and Britten, probably partly due to their own recital experience with folksongs, were naturally interested. They gave the premiere at the 1950 Aldeburgh Festival.

Working on a Britten publication has been a dream come true for me. I would like to thank the following for their kind assistance in making this collection a reality: Colin Matthews of the Britten Estate Limited, Janis Susskind and David Bray of Boosey & Hawkes Music Publishers Ltd., Chris Grogan of the Britten-Pears Library, Faber Music for allowing the use of *Eight Folksongs*, and assistant editors Joel Boyd and Christopher Ruck.

Richard Walters
Editor
July, 2006

[1] Humphrey Carter, *Benjamin Britten: A Biography*
(New York: Charles Scribner's Sons, 1992), 142.

[2] Carter, *Benjamin Britten*, 142.

[3] Carter, *Benjamin Britten*, 154.

[4] Paul Kildea (ed.), *Britten on Music*
(Oxford: Oxford University Press, 2003), 32.

[5] Benjamin Britten, *On Receiving the First Aspen Award*
(London: Faber & Faber, 1964).

[6] Kildea, *Britten on Music*, 63.

[7] Imogen Holst, *Britten* (London: Faber & Faber, 1980), 21-22.

NOTES ON THE SONGS

A principal source for much of the information in this section:

Benjamin Britten: A Catalogue of the Published Works,
compiled and edited by Paul Banks,
published by The Britten-Pears Library for the Britten Estate Limited

Recordings involving Benjamin Britten as pianist are cited. Not all of these are necessarily in current release. In addition, some broadcasts involving Britten as performer might have been released as recordings at some point. Many further recordings by many artists have been made of various Folksong Arrangements over the decades; a discography, which by nature would become dated, was thought to be out of the scope of this publication.

FOLKSONG ARRANGEMENTS
Volume 1: British Isles

Arrangements composed October 1941 (?), 1942. High Voice (original) published by Boosey & Hawkes, 1943. Medium Voice transposed edition published by Boosey & Hawkes, 1946.

Other Britten compositions from this period: *An American Overture* (orchestra, October 1941); *Scottish Ballad*, Op. 26 (two pianos, orchestra, July-October 1941); "What's in your mind?" (high voice, piano, 1941); "Underneath the abject willow" (high voice, piano, 1941); *Hymn to St. Cecilia*, Op. 27 (SSATB chorus, April 1942); "Wild with passion" (high voice, piano, April 1942); "If thou wilt ease thine heart" (high voice, piano, April 1942); arrangement of the song "The Trout" ("Die Forelle") by Schubert (voice, orchestra, June 1942); "Cradle Song" (high voice, piano 1942); *A Ceremony of Carols* (treble chorus, harp, March-October 1942)

The Salley Gardens

Text by William Butler Yeats. The tune is "The Maids of Mourne Shorne." Published source for the melody: *The Complete Collection of Irish Music*, collected by George Petrie, edited by C.V. Stanford. First known performance: Peter Pears, tenor, Benjamin Britten, piano, 26 November 1941, First (Park) Congregational Church, Grand Rapids, Michigan. Recorded by Britten and Pears, 1944, 1954 (both for Decca), 1972 (BBC/IMG). Pears recorded the arrangement with Osian Ellis, harp, 1976 (Decca). Britten transcribed this setting for high voice and string orchestra, first performed by Peter Pears and the New London Orchestra, Alex Sherman, conductor, 13 December 1942, London. Britten also created a version for voice and fuller orchestra in 1955. Both orchestrated versions are included in the study score *Fourteen Folksongs Arranged for Voice and Orchestra* (Boosey & Hawkes); performance materials are available on rental from Boosey & Hawkes. Britten also adapted his arrangement for unison voices and piano.

Dedicated to Clytie Mundy, a voice teacher in New York with whom Peter Pears made remarkable progress.

In the Medium Voice (transposed) previously released publication of Volume 1:

m. 1   Commodo ♩ = 66 (Flowing ♩ = 76 in original High Voice edition)

m. 1   *sempre sostenuto* appears only in Medium Voice

m. 4   *sempre **p** e legato* (*smooth* in High Voice)

m. 23   *più sonore* (*warmer* in High Voice)

Little Sir William

First known performance: Peter Pears, tenor, Benjamin Britten, piano, 26 November 1941, First (Park) Congregational Church, Grand Rapids, Michigan. Recorded by Britten and Pears, 1944, 1954 (both for Decca). Pears recorded the arrangement with Osian Ellis, harp, 1976 (Decca). Britten's orchestrated version was first performed by Peter Pears and the New London Orchestra, Alex Sherman, conductor, 13 December 1942, London. The orchestrated version is included in the study score *Fourteen Folksongs Arranged for Voice and Orchestra* (Boosey & Hawkes); performance materials are available on rental from Boosey & Hawkes.

Dedicated to William Mayer, father/husband of the Mayer family of Amityville, New York, German immigrants and great supporters and friends of Britten and Pears; the two lived with the Mayers for an extended time while on Long Island. Britten dedicated *Hymn to St. Cecilia* to Elizabeth Mayer, matriarch of the family and a surrogate mother to him.

The original text Britten set includes the line "And the Jew's wife hath me slain." The composer later changed this to "And the School wife hath me slain" when he realized the prejudicial slur in the original line, and subsequently only wanted the revised line sung.

In the Medium Voice (transposed) previously released publication of Volume 1:

m. 1   Allegretto con moto (Lightly in the original High Voice edition)

m. 19   *poco meno mosso* (*slower* in High Voice)

m. 19   *sostenuto* (*sustained* in High Voice)

m. 28   *a tempo* (*with movement* in High Voice)

m. 28   *dolce* is added after **pp**

The Bonny Earl o' Moray

The tune, probably believed by Britten to be folk in origin, is possibly by Malcolm Lawson, c. 1885. First known performance: Peter Pears, tenor, Benjamin Britten, piano, 26 November 1941, First (Park) Congregational Church, Grand Rapids, Michigan. Recorded by Britten and Pears, 1945, 1954, 1961 (all for Decca). Britten's orchestrated version was first performed by Peter Pears and the New London Orchestra, Alex Sherman, conductor, 13 December 1942, London. The orchestrated version is included in the study score *Fourteen Folksongs Arranged for Voice and Orchestra* (Boosey & Hawkes); performance materials are available on rental from Boosey & Hawkes.

Dedicated to Mildred Titley, wife of William Titley, superintendent of the Long Island Home (a psychiatric hospital), with whom Britten and Pears resided for a time in Amityville, New York, because of its close proximity to the small house of the Mayer family, their principal hosts.

In the Medium Voice (transposed) previously released publication of Volume 1:

m. 1   Grave (Solemn march in the original High Voice edition)

m. 15   *caloroso* (*express.* in High Voice)

O can ye sew cushions?

First known performance: Peter Pears, tenor, Benjamin Britten, piano, 14 October 1943, St. Margaret's Church, Lowestoft, England. Apparently not recorded by Britten and Pears together, although Pears recorded the song in 1976 (Decca) in a transcription for voice and harp with Osian Ellis. Britten's orchestrated version was first performed by Helena Cook, soprano and the BBC Midland Light Orchestra, Rae Jenkins, conductor, on 6 November 1944 for a General Forces Programme. The orchestrated version is included in the study score *Fourteen Folksongs Arranged for Voice and Orchestra* (Boosey & Hawkes); performance materials are available on rental from Boosey & Hawkes.

Dedicated to Meg Mundy, a singer and daughter of Clytie Mundy, Pears' New York voice teacher.

In the Medium Voice (transposed) previously released publication of Volume 1:

m. 1   Allegretto con moto (Gently rocking in the original High Voice edition)

m. 21   *poco animato* (*lively, with rhythm* in High Voice)

m. 22   *ritmico* appears only in Medium Voice

The trees they grow so high

First known performance: Anne Marie O'Neill, soprano, Andrew Bryson, piano, 8 February 1950, BBC Scottish Home Service.

Dedicated to Bobby Rothman, a young member of the Rothman family of Long Island, New York, of whom Britten was particularly fond.

In the Medium Voice (transposed) previously released publication of Volume 1:

m. 1   Poco allegretto (With movement in the original High Voice edition)

m. 23   *legatissimo* (*very smooth* in High Voice)

m. 45   *espress. e legatis. sempre* (*always smooth and expressive* in High Voice)

m. 67   *più animato* (*more lively* in High Voice)

m. 111   *come prima* (*as at the start* in High Voice)

m. 120   under the bass clef: *morendo il basso*

m. 129   *senza rall.* (*in time* in High Voice)

The Ash Grove

First known performance: Peter Pears, tenor, Benjamin Britten, piano, 14 December 1941, Southold High School, Long Island, New York. Recorded by Britten and Pears, 1944, 1954, 1961 (all for Decca), 1966, (Melodiya, released 1985). Pears recorded the arrangement with Osian Ellis, harp, 1976 (Decca).

Dedicated to Beata Mayer, one of the young adult children in the Mayer family, who reportedly nursed him in illness. See "Little Sir William."

In the Medium Voice (transposed) previously released publication of Volume 1:

m. 1   *legatissimo* (*very smooth* in original High Voice edition)

m. 4   *legatissimo* (*very smooth* over vocal line in High Voice)

m. 5   (*senza cresc. e dim.*) is added after *sempre* **ppp**

m. 37   *cresc. e più sonore* (*cresc. (more sonorous)* in High Voice)

m. 62   *molto espress.* (*express.* in High Voice)

Oliver Cromwell

First known performance: Peter Pears, tenor, Benjamin Britten, piano, 26 November 1941, First (Park) Congregational Church, Grand Rapids, Michigan. Recorded by Britten and Pears, 1944, 1954 (both for Decca). Britten's orchestrated version was first performed by Peter Pears and the New London Orchestra, Alex Sherman, conductor, 13 December 1942, London. The orchestrated version is included in the study score *Fourteen Folksongs Arranged for Voice and Orchestra* (Boosey & Hawkes); performance materials are available on rental from Boosey & Hawkes. Britten also adapted the setting for unison voices and piano.

Dedicated to Christopher Mayer, son in the Mayer family. See "Little Sir William."

In the Medium Voice (transposed) previously released publication of Volume 1:

m. 1   Vivace (Lively in the original High Voice edition)

m. 5   *pesante* (*heavy* in High Voice)

m. 9   *con forza* (*forceful* in High Voice)

m. 43   **p** *sempre più* (*always softer* in High Voice)

m. 47   *senza rit.* (*always in time* in High Voice)

FOLKSONG ARRANGEMENTS
Volume 2: France

Arrangements composed December 1942. High Voice (original) published by Boosey & Hawkes, 1946. Medium Voice transposed edition published by Boosey & Hawkes, 1947.

First known performance of the complete set: Sophie Wyss, soprano, Gerald Moore, piano, 25 March 1943, National Gallery, London. Two songs were performed prior to that date by Peter Pears and Benjamin Britten (see details below). Britten's sources for the songs are not known.

Dedication: "To my young friends, Arnold and Humphrey Gyde." The boys' mother was Sophie Wyss (Mrs. Arnold Gyde), a Swiss soprano for whom Britten wrote the set. Britten dedicated *Les Illuminations* to her; she premiered *Our Hunting Fathers, On This Island* and *Les Illuminations*, as well as the French folksong arrangements.

Five French Folksongs, for baritone and orchestra, are orchestrated versions of selections from the set, performed in the following order: Fileuse, Le roi s'en va-t'en chasse, La belle est au jardin d'amour, Eho! Eho!, Quand j'étais chez mon père. First known performance: Martial Singher, baritone, Chicago Symphony Orchestra, Fritz Busch, conductor, 23 December 1948, Orchestra Hall, Chicago. The orchestrated versions are included in the study score *Fourteen Folksongs Arranged for Voice and Orchestra* (Boosey & Hawkes); performance materials are available on rental from Boosey & Hawkes.

Other Britten compositions from this period: *A Ceremony of Carols* (treble chorus, harp, March-October 1942); *Now sleeps the crimson petal* (tenor, horn, strings, completed March 1943); *Serenade*, Op. 31 (tenor, horn, strings, March-April 1943)

La Noël passée (The Orphan and King Henry)

Britten was not involved in any known recording of this song. At some unknown date Britten transcribed this setting for voice and string orchestra; the song was not included in the 1948 orchestrated set *Five French Folksongs* (see above). The orchestrated version is included in the study score *Fourteen Folksongs*

Arranged for Voice and Orchestra (Boosey & Hawkes); performance materials are available on rental from Boosey & Hawkes.

Voici le printemps (Hear the voice of Spring)

Recorded by Sophie Wyss, soprano, and Benjamin Britten, piano, 1943 (released by EMI, 1993).

Fileuse

Recorded by Sophie Wyss, soprano, and Benjamin Britten, piano, 1943 (released by EMI, 1993). Recorded by Peter Pears, Osian Ellis, harp, 1976 (Decca). See note from previous page on *Five French Folksongs*.

Le roi s'en va-t'en chasse (The King is gone a-hunting)

Recorded by Sophie Wyss, soprano, and Benjamin Britten, piano, 1944 (Decca). Recorded (in English) by Peter Pears, tenor, and Benjamin Britten, piano, 1950 (HMV). Recorded (in French) by Peter Pears, tenor, and Benjamin Britten, piano, 1961 (Decca), 1966 (Melodiya). See note from previous page on *Five French Folksongs*.

La belle est au jardin d'amour (Beauty in love's garden)

First known performance: Peter Pears, tenor, Benjamin Britten, piano, 28 February 1943, Friends House, Euston Road, London. Recorded by Sophie Wyss, soprano, and Benjamin Britten, piano, 1944 (Decca). Recorded by Peter Pears, tenor, and Benjamin Britten, piano, 1961(Decca). Pears recorded the arrangement with Osian Ellis, harp, 1976 (Decca). See note from previous page on *Five French Folksongs*.

Il est quelqu'un sur terre (There's someone in my fancy)

Recorded by Peter Pears, tenor, and Osian Ellis, harp, 1976 (Decca).

Eho! Eho!

Britten or Pears were not involved in any known recording of the song. See note from previous page on *Five French Folksongs*.

Quand j'étais chez mon père (Heigh ho! heigh hi!)

First known performance: Peter Pears, tenor, Benjamin Britten, piano, 28 February 1943, Friends House, Euston Road, London. Recorded by Sophie Wyss, soprano, and Benjamin Britten, piano, 1943 (released by EMI, 1993). Recorded (in English) by Peter Pears, tenor, and Benjamin Britten, piano, 1945 (Decca). See note from previous page on *Five French Folksongs*.

FOLKSONG ARRANGEMENTS
Volume 3: British Isles

Arrangements composed from sometime in 1945 to October, 1946. High Voice (original) published by Boosey & Hawkes, 1948. Medium Voice transposed edition published by Boosey & Hawkes, 1948.

Dedicated to Joan Cross (1900-1993), British soprano, original performer of several Britten opera roles: Ellen Orford in *Peter Grimes*, Lady Billows in *Albert Herring*, Female Chorus in *The Rape of Lucretia*, Elizabeth in *Gloriana*, Mrs. Grose in *The Turn of the Screw*.

Other Britten compositions from this period: *Peter Grimes* (opera, completed February 1945); *Themes for improvisation* (organ, March-July 1945); *The Holy Sonnets of John Donne* (high voice, piano, August 1945); String Quartet No. 2 in C, Op. 36 (September-October 1945); *This Way to the Tomb* (incidental music to the "Masque and Anti-Masque," soloists, SATB chorus, percussion, piano 4 hands, 1944-October 1945);

"Birthday Song for Erwin" (high voice, piano, October-November 1945); multiple Purcell realizations (voice, piano, November 1945); *The Dark Tower* (music for the radio drama, December 1945); *The Young Person's Guide to the Orchestra*, Op. 34 (orchestra, completed December 1945); Purcell realizations (voice, piano, January-February 1946); *The Rape of Lucretia* (opera, January-May 1946); *Occasional Overture*, Op. 38 (orchestra, July-September 1946); *Prelude and Fugue on a Theme of Vittoria* (organ, September 1946); Purcell realisations: *Suite of Songs from Orpheus Britannicus* (high voice, orchestra, before October 1946)

The Plough Boy

Arrangement composed before 27 September 1945. First known performance: Peter Pears, tenor, Benjamin Britten, piano, 27 September 1945, Melksham Music Club, Melksham House, Melksham, England. Recorded by Britten and Pears, 1947 (HMV), 1959 (BBC/IMG), 1961 (Decca), 1963 (Melodiya, live, released 1985), 1972 (Aldeburgh Festival—Snape Maltings Foundation, released 1980). Pears recorded the arrangement with Osian Ellis, harp, 1976 (Decca). Britten's orchestration for voice, flute, string quartet was first performed by Peter Pears, tenor, John Francis, flute, and the Zorian Quartet on 21 November 1946, BBC Light Programme. The orchestrated version is included in the study score *Fourteen Folksongs Arranged for Voice and Orchestra* (Boosey & Hawkes); performance materials are available on rental from Boosey & Hawkes. Britten also used this song (in a different setting) in the score for the 1936 documentary film *Around the Village Green*.

In the Medium Voice (transposed) previously released publication of Volume 3:

m. 1   Allegretto (Quick and gay in original High Voice edition)

m. 1   *non legato* appears only in Medium Voice

m. 1   *sempre staccatissimo* (*always very staccato* in High Voice)

m. 9   *non leggiero* (*lightly* in High Voice)

m. 9   (*staccatissimo*) (*very staccato* in High Voice)

m. 18   *simile* (*sim.* in High Voice)

m. 59   *simile* (*sim.* in High Voice)

m. 91   *non legato* (*staccato* in High Voice)

There's none to soothe

First known performance: Peter Pears, tenor, Benjamin Britten, piano, 27 September 1945, Melksham Music Club, Melksham House, Melksham, England. Recorded by Britten and Pears, 1946, 1954 (both for Decca). Pears recorded the arrangement with Osian Ellis, harp, 1976 (Decca).

In the Medium Voice (transposed) previously released publication of Volume 3:

m. 1   Adagio (Very slow in original High Voice edition)

m. 1   *sonoro* (*sonorous* in High Voice)

Sweet Polly Oliver

First known performance: Peter Pears, tenor, Benjamin Britten, piano, 26 September 1945, Grammar School, Bristol, England. Recorded by Britten and Pears, 1946, 1954, 1961 (all for Decca). Pears recorded the arrangement with Osian Ellis, harp, 1976 (Decca).

In the Medium Voice (transposed) previously released publication of Volume 3:

m. 1   Allegretto (♩) (With movement in original High Voice edition)

m. 1   *chiaro* (*clearly* in High Voice)

m. 24   *poco marc.* (*marked* in High Voice)

m. 44   *sempre stacc.* (*sim.* in High Voice)

m. 60   *poco esitando* (*hesitating* in High Voice)

m. 79   *dolce* (*sweetly* in High Voice)

The Miller of Dee

First known performance: Peter Pears, tenor, Benjamin Britten, piano, 11 March 1946, National Gallery, London. Recorded by Britten and Pears, 1954, 1961 (both for Decca), 1972 (Aldeburgh Festival—Snape Maltings Foundation, released 1980).

In the Medium Voice (transposed) previously released publication of Volume 3:

m. 1   Moderato e ritmico (Slow and steady in original High Voice edition)

m. 2   *poco pesante* (*rather heavy* in High Voice)

m. 11   *pesante* (*heavy* in High Voice)

m. 18   *poco più sonoro* (*with more sound* in High Voice)

m. 18   *marc.* (*marked* in High Voice)

m. 19   *più f e pesante* (*louder* in High Voice)

m. 28   *pesante* (*heavy* in High Voice)

m. 37   *come prima* (*like the start* in High Voice)

m. 46   *pesante* (*heavy* in High Voice)

The Foggy, Foggy Dew

First known performance: Peter Pears, tenor, Benjamin Britten, piano, 27 September 1945, Melksham Music Club, Melksham House, Melksham, England. Recorded by Britten and Pears, 1947 (HMV), 1959 (Decca), 1972 (Aldeburgh Festival—Snape Maltings Foundation, released 1980). Pears recorded the arrangement with Osian Ellis, harp, 1976 (Decca).

In the Medium Voice (transposed) previously released publication of Volume 3:

m. 1   Andante molto comodo (Slow and regular in original High Voice edition)

m. 2   *espress.* (*express.* in High Voice)

m. 5   *simile* (*sim.* in High Voice)

m. 7   *espress.* (*express.* in High Voice)

m. 11   *espress.* (*express.* in High Voice)

m. 24   *espress.* (*express.* in High Voice)

m. 28   *espress.* (*express.* in High Voice)

m. 37   in vocal line: *morendo* (*dying away* in High Voice)

m. 37   in piano part: *morendo* appears only in Medium Voice

O Waly, Waly

First known performance: Peter Pears, tenor, Benjamin Britten, piano, 31 October 1946, Kleine Zaal, Concertgebouw, Amsterdam. Recorded by Britten and Pears, 1950 (HMV), 1961 (Decca). The date of Britten's orchestrated version is not known, nor is its first performance. The orchestrated version is included in the study score *Fourteen Folksongs Arranged for Voice and Orchestra* (Boosey & Hawkes); performance materials are available on rental from Boosey & Hawkes.

In the Medium Voice (transposed) previously released publication of Volume 3:

m. 1   Allegretto (Slowly moving (♩) in original High Voice edition)

m. 1   *espress.* (*express.* in High Voice)

Come you not from Newcastle?

First known performance: Joan Cross, soprano, Nina Milkina, piano, 21 February 1946, BBC Light Programme. Recorded by Britten and Pears, 1947 (HMV), 1961 (Decca). Pears recorded the arrangement with Osian Ellis, harp, 1976 (Decca). Britten orchestrated the arrangement c. 1959; first performance is not known. The orchestrated version is included in the study score *Fourteen Folksongs Arranged for Voice and Orchestra* (Boosey & Hawkes); performance materials are available on rental from Boosey & Hawkes.

In the High Voice previously released publication of Volume 3:

m. 1-2   in piano part: two extra measures appear only in original High Voice edition; they contain the same notes and rhythms as m. 3-4

In the Medium Voice (transposed) previously released publication of Volume 3:

m. 1   Allegro spiritoso (Fast, with spirit in original High Voice edition)

m. 34   *più pp* (m. 36 *pp* in High Voice)

FOLKSONG ARRANGEMENTS
Volume 4: Moore's Irish Melodies

Arrangements composed 1957. High Voice (original) published by Boosey & Hawkes, 1948.

This note from Britten appeared in the original publication:

All the texts of these songs are from Thomas Moore's *Irish Melodies*, published between 1808 and 1834—in one case from the slightly later *National Melodies*. In most instances I have also taken the tunes from the same sources (music arranged by Sir John Stevenson); however, in a few cases I have preferred to go back to Bunting's *Ancient Music of Ireland*, which had in the first place inspired Tom Moore to write his lyrics.

Dedicated to Anthony Gishford, a longtime friend and an employee at Boosey & Hawkes who organized Britten's business affairs.

Other Britten compositions from this period: *Songs from the Chinese* (high voice, guitar, autumn, 1957); Purcell realization: "How blest are shepherds" (high voice, piano, before March 1958); *Noye's Fludde* (opera, October 1957-March 1958)

Avenging and bright

Original tune to which Moore set his words: "Crooghan a venee." First known performance: Peter Pears, tenor, Benjamin Britten, piano, January 1958, Victoria and Albert Museum, London. Recorded by Britten and Pears, 1961 (Decca).

Sail on, sail on

Original tune to which Moore set his words: "The Humming of the Ban." First performance: not known.

How sweet the answer

Original tune to which Moore set his words: "The Wren." Moore's title was "Echoes." First known performance: Peter Pears, tenor, Benjamin Britten, piano, 23 April 1957, Mozartsaal, Konzerthaus, Vienna. Recorded by Britten and Pears, 1961 (Decca). Pears recorded the arrangement with Osian Ellis, harp, 1976 (Decca).

The Minstrel Boy

Original tune to which Moore set his words: "The Moreen." First known performance: Peter Pears, tenor, Benjamin Britten, piano, 23 April 1957, Mozartsaal, Konzerthaus, Vienna. Recorded by Britten and Pears, 1961 (Decca). Pears recorded the arrangement with Osian Ellis, harp, 1976 (Decca).

At the mid hour of night

Original tune to which Moore set his words: "Molly, my Dear." First performance: not known.

Rich and rare

Original tune to which Moore set his words: "The Summer is coming." Moore's title was "Rich and rare were the gems she wore." First performance: not known.

Dear Harp of my Country!

Original tune to which Moore set his words: "Kate Tyrrel." First performance: not known.

Oft in the stilly night

Moore's title was "The Light of Other Days." First known performance: Peter Pears, tenor, Benjamin Britten, piano, January 1958, Victoria and Albert Museum, London. Recorded by Britten and Pears, 1961 (Decca). Pears recorded the arrangement with Osian Ellis, harp, 1976 (Decca).

The last rose of summer

Original tune to which Moore set his words: "Groves of Blarney." First known performance: Peter Pears, tenor, Benjamin Britten, piano, January 1958, Victoria and Albert Museum, London. Recorded by Britten and Pears, 1961 (Decca). Pears recorded the arrangement with Osian Ellis, harp, 1976 (Decca).

O the sight entrancing

Original tune to which Moore set his words: "Planxty Sudley." First performance: not known.

FOLKSONG ARRANGEMENTS
Volume 5: British Isles

Arrangements composed 1951-59. High Voice (original) published by Boosey & Hawkes, 1961.

Composition of these arrangements was scattered through the 1950s. See each song for other Britten compositions from the period.

The Brisk Young Widow

First known performance: Peter Pears, tenor, Benjamin Britten, piano, 24 January 1954, Victoria and Albert Museum, London. Recorded by Britten and Pears, 1954, 1961 (both for Decca).

Other Britten compositions from this period: *Symphonic Suite on Gloriana*, Op. 53a (orchestra, September-December 1953); revision of *Diversions*, Op. 21 (piano left hand, orchestra, 1954); *Am stram gram* (unison voices, piano or four voices unaccompanied, January 1954)

Sally in our Alley

First known performance: Peter Pears, tenor, Benjamin Britten, piano, 22 June 1959, Jubilee Hall, Aldeburgh Festival, Aldeburgh, England. Recorded by Britten and Pears, 1959 (Decca), 1959 (BBC/IMG).

Other Britten compositions from this period: *Fanfare for St. Edmundsbury* (three trumpets, May 1959); Missa Brevis in D, Op. 63 (treble chorus, organ, May 1959); realisation of Charles Dibdin's "Tom Bowling" (high voice, piano, June 1959); multiple Purcell realisations (voice, piano, summer 1959)

The Lincolnshire Poacher

First known performance: Peter Pears, tenor, Benjamin Britten, piano, 22 June 1959, Jubilee Hall, Aldeburgh Festival, Aldeburgh, England. Recorded by Britten and Pears, 1959 (Decca), 1959 (BBC/IMG).

Other Britten compositions from this period: *Fanfare for St. Edmundsbury* (three trumpets, May 1959); Missa Brevis in D, Op. 63 (treble chorus, organ, May 1959); realization of Charles Dibdin's "Tom Bowling" (high voice, piano, June 1959); multiple Purcell realisations (voice, piano, summer 1959)

Early one morning

First known performance: Peter Pears, tenor, Benjamin Britten, piano, 23 April 1957, Mozartsaal, Konzerthaus, Vienna. Recorded by Britten and Pears, 1961 (Decca). Pears recorded the arrangement with Osian Ellis, harp, 1976 (Decca). Britten also used this song (in a different setting) in the score for the 1936 documentary film *Village Harvest*.

Other Britten compositions from this period: *The Prince of the Pagodas* (ballet, early 1955 – autumn 1956); "The Holly and the Ivy" (SATB chorus, July 1957)

Ca' the yowes

First known performance: Peter Pears, tenor, Benjamin Britten, piano, 9 April 1951, Mozartsaal, Konzerthaus, Vienna. Recorded by Britten and Pears, 1961 (Decca). Pears recorded the arrangement with Osian Ellis, harp, 1976 (Decca).

Other Britten compositions from this period: realization of Purcell: *Dido and Aeneas* (opera, completed spring 1951); realization of Purcell: "I take no pleasure" (voice, piano, June 1951); *Six Metamorphoses after Ovid*, Op. 49 (oboe solo, June 1951); *Billy Budd* (opera, January 1950 – November 1951)

FOLKSONG ARRANGEMENTS
Volume 6: England

Arrangements, for high voice and guitar, composed from sometime in 1956 to October 1958 (?). Published by Boosey & Hawkes, 1961. Guitar part edited by Julian Bream.

The editor has made transcriptions for voice and piano for this edition.

Other Britten compositions from this period: Antiphon (chorus, organ, March 1956), *Three Songs from "The Heart of the Matter"* (tenor, horn, piano, May 1956), *The Prince of the Pagodas* (ballet, early 1955-autumn 1956), *Songs from the Chinese* (high voice, guitar, autumn 1957), *Noye's Fludde* (opera, October 1957-March 1958), *Sechs Hölderlin-Fragmente* (high voice, piano, summer 1958), *Nocturne* (tenor, orchestra, August-September 1958)

I will give my love an apple

First known performance: Peter Pears, tenor, Julian Bream, guitar, 6 May 1956, Wigmore Hall, London. Recorded by Pears and Bream, 1963 (RCA), 1977 (DVC). Pears also recorded the song with Osian Ellis, harp, 1976 (Decca).

Sailor-boy

First known performance: Peter Pears, tenor, Julian Bream, guitar, 17 June 1958, Great Glemham House, Aldeburgh Festival, Aldeburgh, England. Recorded by Pears and Bream, 1963 (RCA). Pears also recorded the song with Osian Ellis, harp, 1976 (Decca).

Master Kilby

First known performance: Peter Pears, tenor, Julian Bream, guitar, 17 June 1958, Great Glemham House, Aldeburgh Festival, Aldeburgh, England. Recorded by Pears and Bream, 1963 (RCA), 1977 (DVC). Pears also recorded the song with Osian Ellis, harp, 1976 (Decca).

The Soldier and the Sailor

First known performance: Peter Pears, tenor, Julian Bream, guitar, 6 May 1956, Wigmore Hall, London. Recorded by Pears and Bream, 1963 (RCA). Pears also recorded the song with Osian Ellis, harp, 1976 (Decca).

Bonny at Morn

First performance: not known. In 1976 Britten composed a different arrangement of the song, for voice and harp.

The Shooting of His Dear

First known performance: Peter Pears, tenor, Julian Bream, guitar, 6 May 1956, Wigmore Hall, London. Recorded by Pears and Bream, 1963 (RCA).

EIGHT FOLKSONG ARRANGEMENTS (1976)

Arrangements for high voice and harp composed April-June 1976. Published by Faber Music, 1980. The transcription for medium voice (transposed) and piano by Colin Matthews published by Faber Music, 1980.

Peter Pears and harpist Osian Ellis performed these songs beginning in 1976. Because the selections were often announced from the stage as encores, no record of first performance exists for some.

Eight Folksong Arrangements are included in this collection with the permission of Faber Music Ltd.

Other Britten compositions from this period: String Quartet No. 3, Op. 94 (October-December 1975), *Tema "Sacher"* (solo cello, January 1976), orchestration of Lacrymae, Op. 48 (viola, orchestra, February 1976), realization of William Croft: "A Hymn on Divine Musick (high voice, harp, March 1976), realization of Jeremiah Clarke: "A Divine Hymn (high voice, harp, 1975-mid 1976), realization of Pelham Humfrey: Hymn to God the Father; Lord! I have sinned" (high voice, harp or piano, 1975-mid 1976), *Welcome Ode* (treble chorus, orchestra, summer 1976), *Praise We Great Men* (soloists, chorus, orchestra, July-October 1976)

Lord! I married me a wife

First performance: not known. Recorded by Peter Pears, tenor, Osian Ellis, harp, 1977 (Decca). Published source for the melody and words: *English Folksongs from the Southern Appalachians Volume II*, collected by Cecil Sharp, edited by Maud Karpeles, Second Edition, (Oxford University Press, 1932). The original title of the song was "Rain and Snow." The song was documented from the singing of Mrs. Tom Rice, Big Laurel, North Carolina, 18 August 1916.

She's like the swallow

First known performance: Peter Pears, tenor, Osian Ellis, harp, 17 June 1976, Snape Maltings Concert Hall, Aldeburgh Festival, Aldeburgh, England. Recorded by Peter Pears, tenor, Osian Ellis, harp, 1977 (Decca). Published source for the melody and words: *Folksongs from Newfoundland*, collected by Maud Karpeles (London: Faber & Faber, 1971). Karpeles documented the song from the singing of John Hunt, Dunville, Placentia Bay, 8 July 1930. Words and melody © 1971 by Faber & Faber Ltd. Reprinted with permission.

Lemady

First known performance: Peter Pears, tenor, Osian Ellis, harp, 10 November 1977, Mandel Hall, University of Chicago. Published source for the melody and words: *Journal of the Folksong Society*, Volume V, No. 19, June 1915. The song was documented by Clive Carey from the singing of Robert Beadle at Stoup Brow, Whitby, Yorkshire, England, September 1911. Words and melody © 1915 by J. Curwen & Sons Ltd. Reprinted with permission.

Bonny at Morn

First performance: not known. Source: *North Countrie Ballads, Songs and Pipe Tunes*, arranged by W. Gillies Whittaker (London: J. Curwen & Sons, 1885). Britten's voice and guitar arrangement of this song, dissimilar but related to the voice and harp arrangement, was composed in the 1950s as part of *Folksong Arrangements Volume 6: England*.

I was lonely and forlorn (Bugeilio'r Gwenith Gwyn)

First performance: not known. Traditional Welsh Air. Published source for the melody and words: *Ancient National Airs of Gwent and Morgannwg* (1844), collected by Maria Jane Williams of Aberpergwn. English words by Osian Ellis. Reprinted with permission.

David of the White Rock (Dafydd y Garreg Wen)

First performance: not known. Melody by David Owen (1709-39) of "Y Garreg Wen" near Porthmadog, Gwynnedd. Published in *Musical and Poetical Relicks of the Welsh Bards* (1784). Welsh words by Ceiriog (John Ceiriog Hughes, 1832-87); second verse added by Osian Ellis. English words by Thomas Oliphant (translated from a Welsh lyric by Talhaiarn), published in Hullah's *The Song Book* (London: Macmillan, 1866).

The False Knight upon the Road

First known performance: Peter Pears, tenor, Osian Ellis, harp, 10 November 1977, Mandel Hall, University of Chicago. Published source for the melody and words: *English Folksongs from the Southern Appalachians*, collected by Cecil Sharp, edited by Maud Karpeles, Second Edition, (Oxford University Press, 1932). The song was documented from the singing of Mrs. T.G. Coates at Flag Pond, Tennessee, 1 September 1916.

Bird Scarer's Song

First known performance: Peter Pears, tenor, Osian Ellis, harp, 17 June 1976, Snape Maltings Concert Hall, Aldeburgh Festival, Aldeburgh, England. Published source for the melody and words: *Journal of the Folksong Society*, Volume II, No. 6, January 1905. The song was documented from the singing of John Parnell at East Harptree, Somerset, England, April 1904. The original title of the song was "Bird Starver's Cry."

TOM BOWLING AND OTHER SONG ARRANGEMENTS

This volume of various song arrangements, previously unpublished, was released by Boosey & Hawkes, 2001. The title of the collection was given by the publisher, as was the original published order of the songs, retained here.

Tom Bowling

Words and music by Charles Dibdin (1745-1814), written for the ballad opera (or "table entertainment") *The Oddities* (1789). Original key: High Voice. Britten's realization composed sometime before June 1959. First known performance: Peter Pears, tenor, Benjamin Britten, piano, June 1959, Jubilee Hall, Aldeburgh Festival, Aldeburgh, England. Recorded by Britten and Pears, 1959 (BBC/IMG), 1959 (Decca). Britten and Pears performed the song for years before the composer wrote this realization. Though this is not a folksong, its inclusion in this collection is logical due to its appearance in the publication *Tom Bowling and Other Song Arrangements*.

Other Britten compositions from this period: *Fanfare for St. Edmundsbury* (three trumpets, May 1959); Missa Brevis in D, Op. 63 (treble chorus, organ, May 1959); folksong arrangements of "Salley in our Alley" and "The Lincolnshire Poacher" (high voice, piano, June 1959); multiple Purcell realizations (voice, piano, summer 1959)

The Crocodile

Arrangement composed sometime before December 1941. First known performance: Peter Pears, tenor, Benjamin Britten, piano, 14 December 1941, Southold High School, Long Island, New York. Britten's apparent source was *English Country Songs*, collected and edited by L. Broadwood and J.A. Fuller Maitland (London: The Leadenhall Press, 1893).

Other Britten compositions from this period: *An American Overture* (orchestra, October 1941); *Scottish Ballad*, Op. 26 (two pianos, orchestra, July – October 1941); "What's in your mind?" (high voice, piano, 1941) ; "Underneath the abject willow" (high voice, piano, 1941); from *Folksong Arrangements Volume 1: British Isles*: "The Salley Gardens," "Little Sir William," "The Bonny Earl o' Moray," "Oliver Cromwell" (high voice, piano, October – November 1941); arrangements of "Greensleeves," "I wonder as I wander" (high voice, piano, 1941?)

Dink's Song

The date of the voice and piano arrangement is unknown, as is its first performance. Britten's apparent source was *American Ballads and Folksongs*, collected and compiled by John A. Lomax and Alan Lomax (New York: Macmillan, 1934).

Greensleeves

Arrangement composed 1941(?). This famous English tune, dating back, first mentioned in the "Stationers' Register" 1580, has had various versions. Britten's source is unknown. First performance: not known.

Other Britten compositions from this period: *An American Overture* (orchestra, October 1941); *Scottish Ballad*, Op. 26 (two pianos, orchestra, July-October 1941); "What's in your mind?" (high voice, piano, 1941); "Underneath the abject willow" (high voice, piano, 1941), from *Folksong Arrangements Volume 1: British Isles:* "The Salley Gardens," "Little Sir William," "The Bonny Earl o' Moray," "Oliver Cromwell" (high voice, piano, October-November 1941); arrangement of "The Crocodile" (high voice, piano, December 1941); arrangement of "I wonder as I wander" (high voice, piano, 1941?)

The Holly and the Ivy

The date of composition of the voice and piano arrangement is unknown. Various versions of the song exist in different sources. Britten also created a completely different unaccompanied SATB arrangement in 1957.

I wonder as I wander

Arrangement composed 1940-41 (?). First performance: not known. The song, apparently an original composition by John Jacob Niles, was published in *Songs of the Hill Folk* (New York: G. Schirmer, 1934). Because of copyright clearance difficulties the arrangement remained unpublished. Britten and Pears performed it regularly, as late as September, 1972.

Other Britten compositions from this period: *An American Overture* (orchestra, October 1941); *Scottish Ballad*, Op. 26 (two pianos, orchestra, July-October 1941); "What's in your mind?" (high voice, piano, 1941) ; "Underneath the abject willow" (high voice, piano, 1941), from *Folksong Arrangements Volume 1: British Isles:* "The Salley Gardens," "Little Sir William," "The Bonny Earl o' Moray," "Oliver Cromwell" (high voice, piano, October – November 1941); arrangement of "The Crocodile" (high voice, piano, December 1941); arrangement of "Greensleeves" (high voice, piano, 1941?)

Pray goody

Arrangement composed 1945-46 (?). First performance: not known. The source for words and melody is John Hullah's *The Song Book* (London: Macmillan, 1866). The song is originally from Kane O'Hara's English burletta *Midas* (Dublin, 1761). The tune for this burletta use was taken from *Queen Mab*, a 1750 pantomime assembled by Henry Woodward. The musical attribution was to "The Society of the Temple of Apollo," Charles Burney's elaborate pseudonym.

Other Britten compositions from this period: *Peter Grimes* (opera, completed February 1945); *Themes for improvisation* (organ, March-July 1945); *The Holy Sonnets of John Donne* (high voice, piano, August 1945); String Quartet No. 2 in C, Op. 36 (September-October 1945); *This Way to the Tomb* (incidental music to the "Masque and Anti-Masque," soloists, SATB chorus, percussion, piano 4 hands, 1944-October 1945); "Birthday Song for Erwin" (high voice, piano, October-November 1945); multiple Purcell realizations (voice, piano, November 1945); *The Dark Tower* (music for the radio drama, December 1945); *The Young Person's Guide to the Orchestra*, Op. 34 (orchestra, completed December 1945); Purcell realizations (voice, piano, January-February 1946); *The Rape of Lucretia* (opera, January-May 1946); *Occasional Overture*, Op. 38 (orchestra, July-September 1946); *Prelude and Fugue on a Theme of Vittoria* (organ, September 1946); Purcell realizations: *Suite of Songs from Orpheus Britannicus* (high voice, orchestra, before October 1946); *Folksong Arrangements Volume 3: British Isles* (high voice, piano, 1945-October 1946)

The Deaf Woman's Courtship

Arrangement for two voices and piano probably composed c. 1958 (?) for recitals by contralto Norma Procter and tenor Peter Pears. First performance: not known. Source: *English Folksongs from the Southern Appalachians*, collected by Cecil Sharp, edited by Maud Karpeles, 2nd edition (Oxford University Press, 1932).

Other Britten compositions from this period: realization of Purcell: "How blest are shepherds" (voice, piano, March 1958); arrangement of "Soldier, won't you marry me?" (two voices, piano, March 1958); *Noye's Fludde* (opera, March 1958); from *Folksong Arrangements Volume 6: England*: "Sailor-boy," "Master Kilby" (high voice, guitar, June 1958); *Sechs Hölderlin-Fragmente* (voice, piano, summer 1958)

Soldier, won't you marry me?

Arrangement for two voices and piano composed sometime before 15 March 1958. First performance: Norma Procter, contralto, Peter Pears, tenor, Benjamin Britten, piano, 15 March 1958, Düsseldorf, Germany. Source: *English Folksongs from the Southern Appalachians*, collected by Cecil Sharp, edited by Maud Karpeles, Second Edition (Oxford University Press, 1932). This setting was originally intended to be included in *Folksong Arrangements Volume 5: British Isles*.

Other Britten compositions from this period: realization of Purcell: "How blest are shepherds" (voice, piano, March 1958); arrangement of "The Deaf Woman's Courtship" (two voices, piano, March 1958); *Noye's Fludde* (opera, March 1958); from *Folksong Arrangements Volume 6: England*: "Sailor-boy," "Master Kilby" (high voice, guitar, June 1958); *Sechs Hölderlin-Fragmente* (voice, piano, summer 1958)

The Stream in the Valley

Arrangement for voice, violoncello, piano composed sometime before 21 November 1946. First known performance: Peter Pears, tenor, Maurice Gendron, violoncello, Benjamin Britten, piano, 21 November 1946, BBC Light Programme. Britten's source for the German folksong is not known.

Other Britten compositions from this period: *The Rape of Lucretia* (opera, January-May 1946); *Occasional Overture*, Op. 38 (orchestra, July-September 1946); *Prelude and Fugue on a Theme of Vittoria* (organ, September 1946); realizations of Purcell: *Suite of Songs from Orpheus Britannicus* (high voice, orchestra, October 1946); *Folksong Arrangements Volume 3: British Isles* (high voice, piano, 1945-October 1946)

Preface

from the Boosey & Hawkes publication
Tom Bowling and Other Song Arrangements

Benjamin Britten's songs in English for the most part fall into three distinct groups: settings of old and modern poetry; arrangements of traditional folksongs; and realizations of songs by Henry Purcell. There were remarkably few deviations from these broad categories.

Even the ten rather disparate songs collected in this volume hardly deviate from the norm. They date from 1941, soon after Britten had begun his great recital partnership with Peter Pears, up to 1959 or so. Exactly why these songs were not published in Britten's lifetime is not always possible to ascertain. Some of them would have fitted happily into other collections: "The Crocodile," "Greensleeves," and "The Holly and the Ivy" are after all English folksongs, and at least the first can be dated to a recital given by Pears and Britten on Long Island, New York, in 1941—exactly the period in which he was arranging the pieces that make up his first volume of folksongs. Similarly, "I wonder as I wander" (1940-41?), "The Deaf Woman's Courtship" (probably arranged in the 1950s for joint recitals by Pears and the contralto Norma Procter) and "Soldier, won't you marry me?" (by 15 March 1958, another duet for the same performers), with some poetic license, could have slotted into an 'English' collection, for although they are considered 'traditional American' songs, they had been taken there by English emigrants seeking a new life in the Southern Appalachians. And perhaps Britten's intention with "The Stream in the Valley" ("Da unten im Tale"), first performed in a BBC broadcast on 21 November 1946 by Pears and Britten with the cellist Maurice Gendron, was to compile a volume of German folksongs to compliment his French collection of 1942—an audacious move in the exuberantly nationalist period immediately following the War, but one wholly typical of this composer.

In most cases, nothing untoward should be read into the fact that Britten did not include particular pieces in the volumes he was then compiling and publishing: he frequently composed songs "surplus to requirement," which were then jettisoned because they didn't fit a precise formal design, rather than through a perceived fault (although it is fair to say that this happened mostly in his song cycles). In certain instances, though there were actual barriers to publication. Before his works were first published in the 1930s, Britten had quite understandably remained largely unaware of issues of copyright. Given that his poetry settings at this stage were remarkably contemporary (he had a genuine enthusiasm for Walter de la Mare), many of his juvenile songs would have required an author royalty had they been published. The few that were (the Three Two-part Songs of 1932, for example) and the commercial terms imposed upon Britten as a result presaged something of an about-turn in the poets and authors he subsequently set. Of course he continued to set contemporary texts and authors, but on the whole he avoided copyright works unless they were those of a friend or collaborator. "I wonder as I wander" was neither, yet Britten's new arrangements of old songs had their own copyright complications. No matter how traditional the original, the contemporary authors, collectors and publishers of any song used as a source of a new setting were eligible for a royalty. Britten's arrangement, possibly made as early as 1940, was based on one by John Jacob Niles, which had been published in *Songs of the Hill Folk* (Schirmer, 1934), and the ensuing wrangling between publishers meant that it was neither issued nor broadcast in his lifetime, although it was often included in his recitals with Pears. "Soldier, won't you marry me?" perhaps suffered a similar fate, for although it was intended for volume 5 of Britten's folksong arrangements (released in 1961), it was dropped at the last moment, following attempts to negotiate a lower royalty agreement with another publisher.

Quite a different fate prevented the issue of "Dink's Song" (date unknown). Prior to this current publication, Britten's arrangement existed simply as a written-out melody and accompaniment, without a title or any underlying words. A version of this song, collected from a black American woman, appears with text in

John and Alan Lomax's *American Ballads and Folksongs* (New York: Macmillan, 1934)—a 1941 edition of which Britten possessed—and although there are slight rhythmic discrepancies between this and Britten's arrangement, pencil markings in his copy and hand suggest that this was indeed his source.

The song that lends its name to this volume, however, could not have found a home in another volume, nor was it conceived as part of a larger cycle or series. "Tom Bowling" was composed by Charles Dibdin (1745-1814) and realized some time before June 1959, when it was first performed by Pears and Britten in the Aldeburgh Festival, although prior to this the original song had often been included in their recital programmes. It is a remarkable miniature—both because it was Britten's first realization of a song by someone other than Purcell (which he followed, in the few years before his death, with realizations of songs by William Croft, Pelham Humfrey, Jeremiah Clarke and John Blow), and because of its narrative content. Few English composers from the 17th and 18th centuries were anywhere near as appealing to Britten as Purcell; their songs lacked his harmonic inventiveness and exquisite word setting. Although the harmonic language of "Tom Bowling" is straightforwardly diatonic, the melismatic vocal line, with its sensitive and colourful setting of the text, lives up to Purcell's example, while the range and placement of the song made it perfectly suited to Pears' voice.

More attractive to Britten, perhaps, than these qualities was the short but poignant story of "Tom Bowling." The real Tom Bowling was Dibdin's brother—lost at sea and much mourned by those who knew him. In the song, Tom's fellow sailors tell us that he was "the darling of our crew...his form was of the manliest beauty, his heart was kind and soft." As such, he is a brother to Billy Budd: a character of beauty and goodness, of great potential and achievement—destroyed in this instance by nature rather than the malevolent forces at work in Britten's opera of 1951. This archetype appears of course in a number of guises in Britten's works; perhaps the closest replication, though, is the Cabin-Boy in *The Golden Vanity* (1966), whose courageous actions save his ship from murderous pirates, but who is then left to drown by the captain and to be mourned by his fellow crew members.

Through its narrative links to other Britten works, through its careful crafting for the voice of Peter Pears, and through its similarities and differences from other arrangements and realizations from this period, "Tom Bowling" suggests a fitting way for us to view the rest of the songs in the collection. These same qualities can be identified in the remaining nine songs, although articulating such links is not an exercise of which Britten himself would have approved: each song was intended as a simple, often humorous, addition to the repertory, an intention this publication honours.

Paul Kildea
Editor of *Tom Bowling and Other Song Arrangements*
© Copyright 2001 by Paul Kildea

FOLKSONG ARRANGEMENTS
Volume 1
British Isles

To Clytie Mundy

The Salley Gardens

Irish Tune

original key

*Words by
W. B. YEATS

Arranged by
BENJAMIN BRITTEN

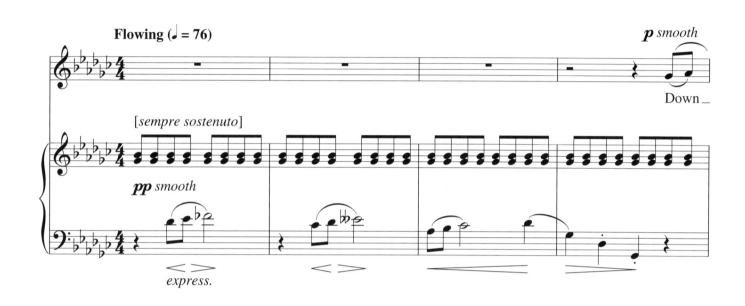

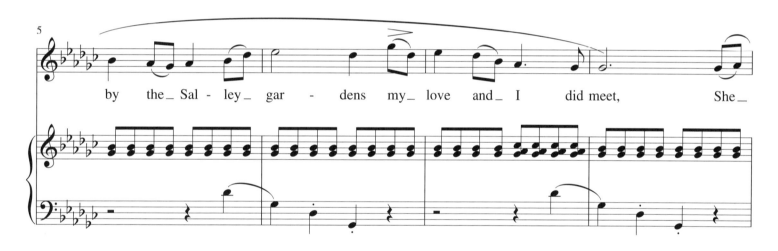

The words of this song are reprinted from "Collected Poems of W. B. Yeats" by permission of Mrs. Yeats.

To William Mayer

Little Sir William

Somerset Folk Song

original key

Arranged by
BENJAMIN BRITTEN

Lightly (♩ = 66)

mf

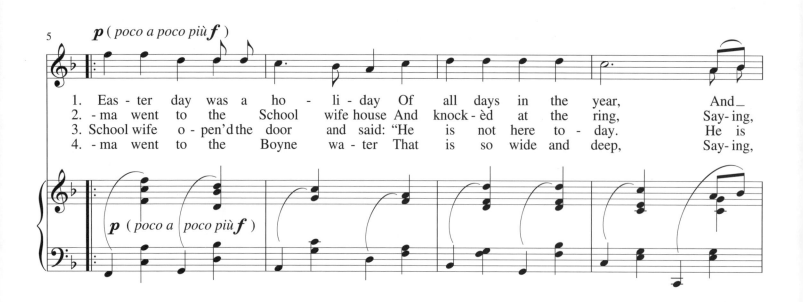

p (*poco a poco più* *f*)

1. Eas - ter day was a ho - li - day Of all days in the year, And
2. -ma went to the School wife house And knock - èd at the ring, Say - ing,
3. School wife o - pen'd the door and said: "He is not here to - day. He is
4. -ma went to the Boyne wa - ter That is so wide and deep, Say - ing,

p (*poco a* | *poco più* *f*)

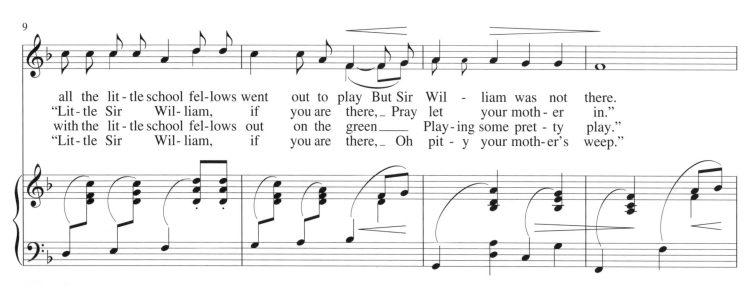

all the lit - tle school fel - lows went out to play But Sir Wil - liam was not there.
"Lit - tle Sir Wil - liam, if you are there,_ Pray let your moth - er in."
with the lit - tle school fel - lows out on the green_ Play - ing some pret - ty play."
"Lit - tle Sir Wil - liam, if you are there,_ Oh pit - y your moth - er's weep."

To Mildred Titley

The Bonny Earl o' Moray

Scottish Tune

original key

Arranged by
BENJAMIN BRITTEN

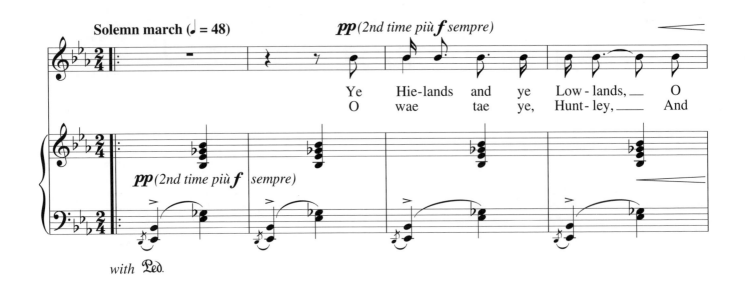

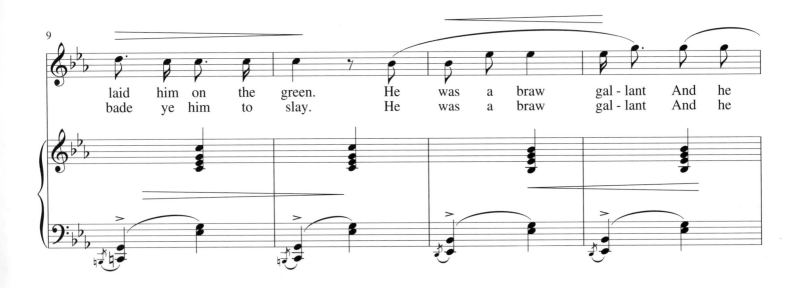

9

To Meg Mundy

O can ye sew cushions?

Scottish Tune

original key

Arranged by
BENJAMIN BRITTEN

To Bobby Rothman

The trees they grow so high

Somerset Folk Song

original key

Arranged by
BENJAMIN BRITTEN

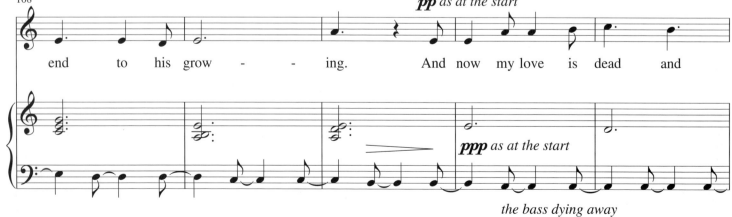

93 *cresc.*

at the age of sev-en-teen he was fa-ther to— a son.— And at the age of

cresc.

f poco

f *express.*

98 *a poco dim.*

eight-een the grass grew o-ver him, Cru-el death soon put— an end to his

dim.

103

grow - - ing, Grow - ing, grow - ing, cru-el death— soon put an

p

p sempre più

marcato

108

end to his grow - - ing. And now my love is dead and

pp as at the start

ppp as at the start

the bass dying away

To Beata Mayer

The Ash Grove

Welsh Tune

original key

Arranged by
BENJAMIN BRITTEN

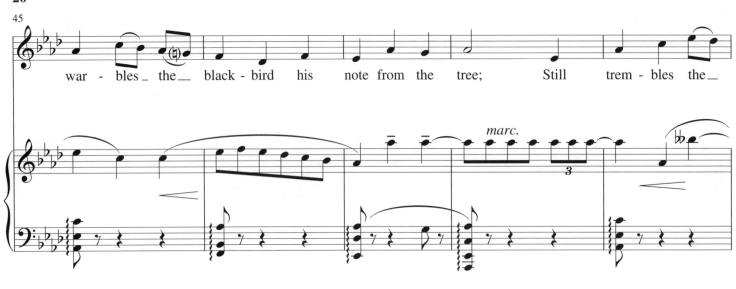

war - bles _ the _ black - bird his note from the tree; Still trem - bles the _

moon - beam on stream - let _ and _ foun - tain, But what are _ the _ beau - ties of

na - ture to me. With sor - row, _ deep _ sor - row, my bos - om _ is _

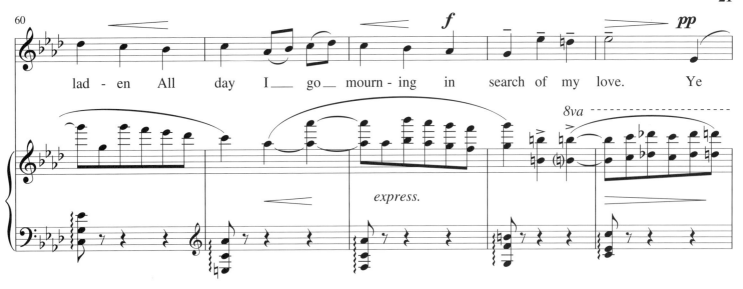

lad - en All day I __ go __ mourn - ing in search of my love. Ye

express.

ech - oes, O tell me, where is the __ sweet __ maid - en? She sleeps 'neath __ the __

green turf down by the Ash - grove.

dim.

molto rall.

To Christopher Mayer

Oliver Cromwell

Nursery Rhyme from Suffolk

original key

Arranged by
BENJAMIN BRITTEN

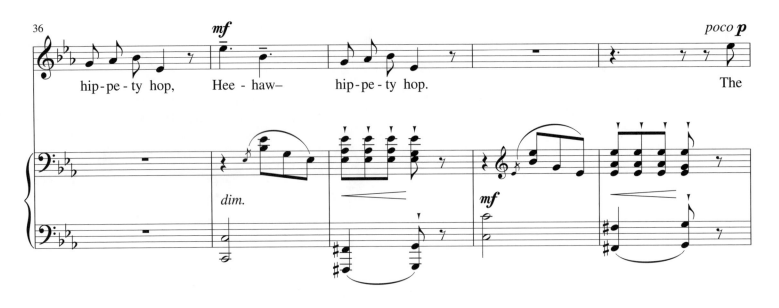

hip-pe - ty hop, Hee - haw— hip-pe - ty hop. The

sad - dle and bri - dle, they lie on the shelf, Hee - haw— lie on the shelf, if you

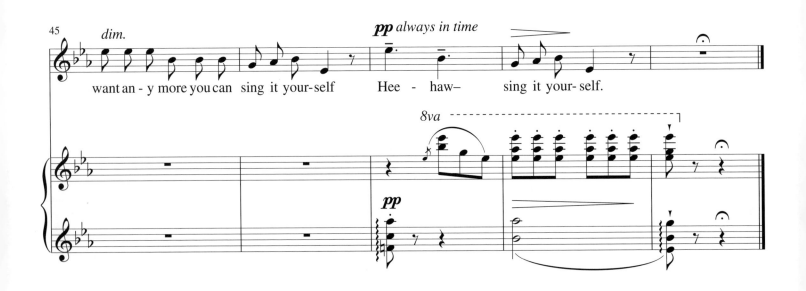

want an - y more you can sing it your-self Hee - haw— sing it your-self.

FOLKSONG ARRANGEMENTS
Volume 2
France

La Noël passée

(The Orphan and King Henry)

original key

English translation by
IRIS ROGERS

Arranged by
BENJAMIN BRITTEN

*If the third verse is omitted, start the fourth verse thus:

Le roi dit: "Pe - tit   ange,
The king said: "Lit - tle   an - gel,

Voici le printemps

(Hear the voice of Spring)

original key

English translation by
IRIS ROGERS

Arranged by
BENJAMIN BRITTEN

1. Voi - ci le prin - temps qui pas - se; "Bon - jour, tis - se - rand bon - jour! A - mi, cè - de moi ta pla - ce, J'en ai be - soin pour un jour. C'est moi qui fait la toi -

1. *Hear the voice of Spring who pass - eth: "Mas - ter Weav - er, here's good - day! May I take thy place," she ask - eth, "For I need it just one day. I must clothe the woods in*

Fileuse

original key

English translation by
IRIS ROGERS

Arranged by
BENJAMIN BRITTEN

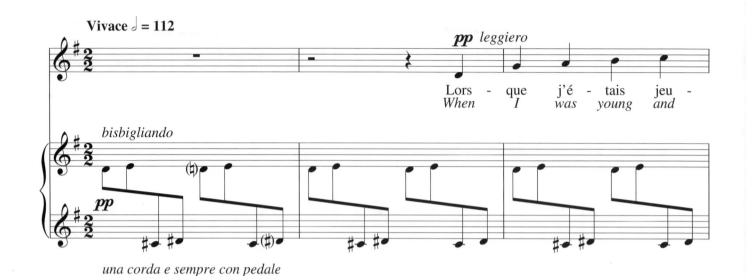

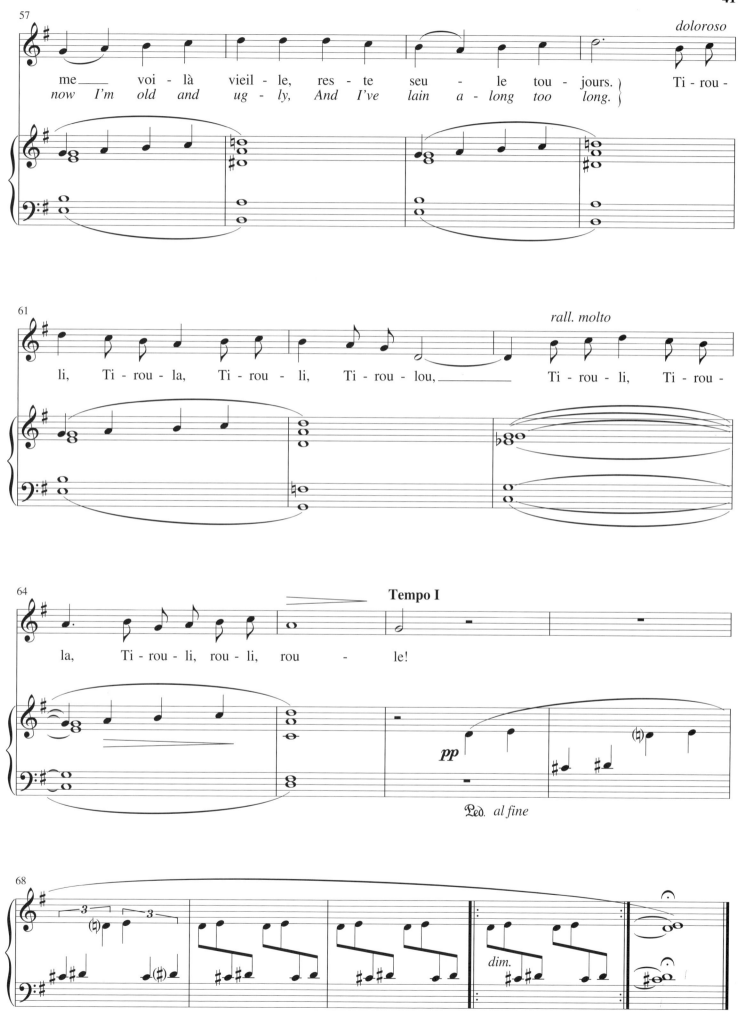

Le roi s'en va-t'en chasse

(The King is gone a-hunting)

original key

English translation by
IRIS ROGERS

Arranged by
BENJAMIN BRITTEN

Poco più lento

3. Ren - contre u - ne ber - gè - re Qui
3. But he's found a shep - herd maid - en A -

dor - mait dans les joncs, Qui dor - mait dans les
sleep be - neath a tree, A - sleep be - neath a

joncs, Mon ai - ma - ble ber - gè - re. Qui
tree, My a - dor - a - ble maid - en: A -

dor - mait dans les joncs, ber - gè - re Na - non.
sleep be - neath a tree, Sweet maid - en Ma - rie.

Tempo I

jons._____ De - dans mes beaux_ don - jons,⎫
son._____ Et de l'or à ____ foi - son,⎬ Mon ai - ma - ble ber - gè - re._____
rons._____ De ducs et de ____ ba - rons)⎭

me, _____ And live in state_ with me?⎫
ty, _____ And gold in quan - ti - ty,⎬ My a - dor - a - ble maid - en._____
dee, _____ Two ba - rons, one ____ gran - dee,⎭

____ De - dans mes beaux_ don jons, ⎫
Et de l'or à ____ foi - son, ⎬ Ber - gè - re Na - non."_____
(De ducs et de ____ ba - rons) ⎭

____ And live in state _ with me? ⎫
____ And gold in quan - ti - ty.) ⎬ Sweet maid-en Ma - rie."_____
(Two ba - rons one ____ gran - dee.) ⎭

La belle est au jardin d'amour

(Beauty in love's garden)
original key

English translation by
IRIS ROGERS

Arranged by
BENJAMIN BRITTEN

Andantino ♩. = 60

poco a poco più agitato

espress.

p

ma poco a poco più agitato

p

pp

1. La belle est au jar - din d'a - mour,   La belle est au
2. Son pè - re la cher - che par - tout,   Son pè - re la
1. Beau-ty in love's gar - den is bound,   Beau-ty in love's
2. Fa-ther is search - ing all a - round,   Fa-ther is search -

jar - din d'a - mour.   Il y'a un mois   ou   cinq se - mai - nes.
cher - che par - tout.   Son a - mou - reux   qui   est en pei - ne.
gar - den is bound.   Full thir - ty nights   and   man - y a morn - ing.
ing all a - round.   And Co - lin weep - eth   for   his dar - ling.)

p

La - ri - don - don,   la - ri - don - dai - ne.
Hey der - ry down,   hey   down a - down - ing.

espress.

Il est quelqu'un sur terre

(There's someone in my fancy)

original key

English translation by
IRIS ROGERS

Arranged by
BENJAMIN BRITTEN

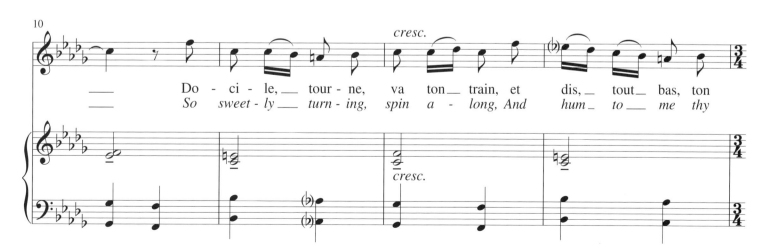

Eho! Eho!

(Eho! Eho!)

original key

English translation by
IRIS ROGERS

Arranged by
BENJAMIN BRITTEN

Poco presto ♩. = 84

Eho!   Eho!   Eho!_____ Les ag-neaux vont aux plai - nes.____
Eho!   Eho!   Eho!_____ Keep your lambs in the val - ley.____

Eho!   Eho!   Eho!_____ Et les loups vont aux bois.____
Eho!   Eho!   Eho!_____ For the wolf's in the wood.____

p (*poco a poco più agitato*)

1. Tant qu'aux bords des fon - tai - nes.____ Ou dans les frais ruis - seaux,
1. The white lambs they do dal - ly,____ By the foun-tain and spring,____

____ Les blancs mou-tons s'y bai - gnent,____ Y dan-sant au pré - au.____
____ As they bathe and skip glad - ly,____ All a-round in a ring.____

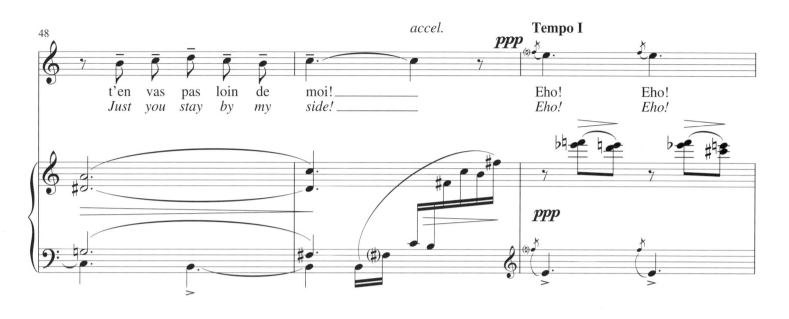

Quand j'étais chez mon père

(Heigh ho, heigh hi!)

original key

English translation by
IRIS ROGERS

Arranged by
BENJAMIN BRITTEN

Con ritmo deliberato (alla Ländler) ♩. = 52

p giocoso

p pesante

1. Quand j'é-
2. Mais je
1. Oh I
2. Oh they

tais chez mon pè - re, ap-pren-ti pas-tou-reau, il m'a mis dans la
n'en a - vais guè - re, je n'a - vais qu'trois a - gneaux; et le loup de la
lived with my dad - dy, An ap - pren - tice was I, Just a poor shep-herd
weren't ver - y man - y, And the lambs they did die, For the wolf swal-lowed

lan - de, pour gar - der les trou - piaux.
plai - ne m'a man - gé le plus biau.
lad - die, to my sheep I did cry.
dai - ly all the best and most spry.

Trou-piaux, trou-piaux, je
Heigh - ho, heigh - hi, they

sonoro

marc.

FOLKSONG ARRANGEMENTS
Volume 3
British Isles

The Plough Boy

Tune by W. Shield

original key

Arranged by
BENJAMIN BRITTEN

great a man I'll be, So great a man, so great a man, so great a man I'll

be, You'll for - get the lit - tle plough - boy who whis - tled o'er the lea,_____ You'll for-

get the lit - tle plough - boy who whis - tled o'er the lea. I'll

buy votes at e - lec - tions, and when I've made the pelf,_____ I'll stand poll for the

There's none to soothe

Hullah's Song Book (Scottish)

original key

Arranged by
BENJAMIN BRITTEN

Sweet Polly Oliver

Old English Tune

original key

Arranged by
BENJAMIN BRITTEN

Then up spoke the ser - geant one day — at his
drill. "Now who's good for nurs - ing? A — cap - tain, he's
ill." "I'm read - y," said Pol - ly — To — nurse him she's
gone, And finds it's her true — love all wast - ed and wan.

if you were his wife." O then Pol - ly Ol-i-ver, she

burst __ in - to tears And told the good doc - tor her __ hopes and her

fears And ver-y short - ly af - ter, __ for __ bet-ter or for worse, The cap-tain took

joy-ful - ly his pret-ty sol - dier nurse.

The Miller of Dee

Hullah's Song Book (English)

original key

Arranged by
BENJAMIN BRITTEN

The Foggy, Foggy Dew

from Suffolk

original key

Arranged by
BENJAMIN BRITTEN

I am a bach-elor and I live with my son, and we work at the weav - er's express.

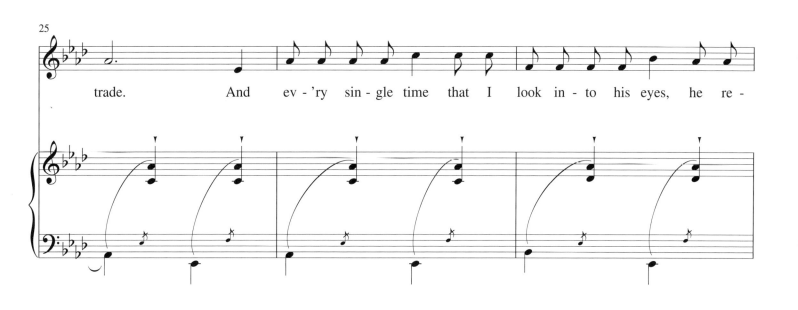

trade. And ev -'ry sin - gle time that I look in - to his eyes, he re -

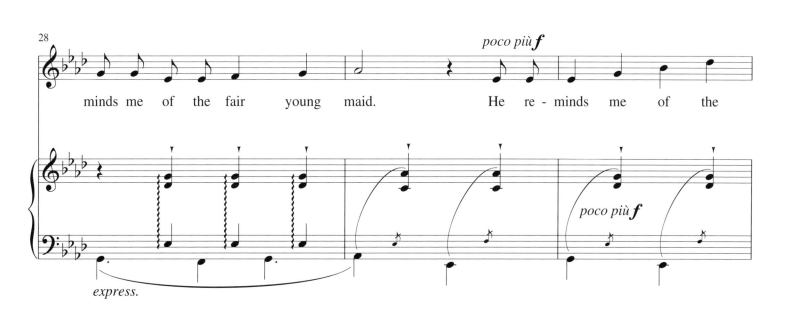

minds me of the fair young maid. He re - minds me of the express.

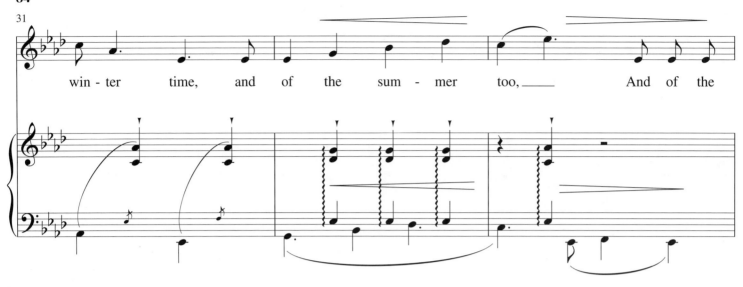

winter time, and of the sum - mer too, _____ And of the

man - y, man - y times that I held her in my arms, just to

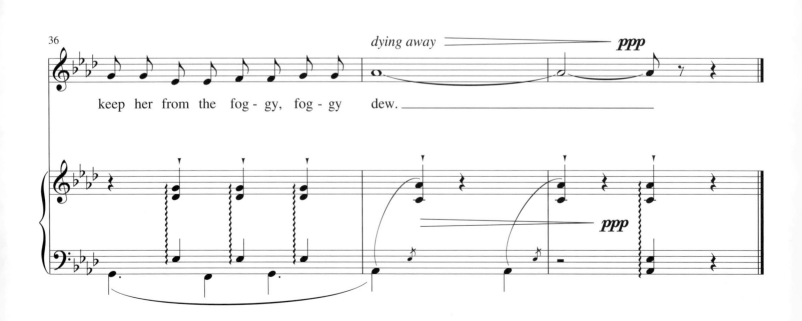

keep her from the fog - gy, fog - gy dew. _____

O Waly, Waly

from Somerset (Cecil Sharp) *

original key

Arranged by
BENJAMIN BRITTEN

Lyrics (verse 1 / verse 2):

The wa-ter is wide I can-not get o'er, and nei-ther have I wings to fly. Give me a boat that will car-ry two, and both shall

I leaned my back up a-gainst some oak think-ing that he was a trust-y tree; But first he bend-ed, and then he broke; and so did

O, love is hand - some and love is fine, and love's a

jew - el while it is new, But when it is old, it grow-eth

cold, and fades a - way like morn-ing dew.

Come you not from Newcastle?

Hullah's Song Book (English)

original key

Arranged by
BENJAMIN BRITTEN

should_ I_ not speed af - ter him, since love to all is free?

Come you not from New - cas - tle?_____

Come you not there a - way?_____ O_ met you not my

true love, _____ rid - ing on a bon - ny bay?_____

Why_ should_ I__ not love my love? __ Why

should not my love__ love__ me?__ Why__

should_ I__ not speed af - ter him,_____ since love to

all is free?_____

FOLKSONG ARRANGEMENTS
Volume 4
Moore's Irish Melodies

Avenging and bright

(*Crooghan a venee*)
original key

from Thomas Moore's *Irish Melodies*

Arranged by
BENJAMIN BRITTEN

wreaked on the mur-der-er's head! *heavy* 4. Yes, mon-arch!_ though_

sweet are our home rec-ol - lec - tions, Though sweet are _ the _ tears that from

ten-der-ness fall; Though sweet are _ our_ friend-ships, our hopes and_ af -

fec-tions, Re - venge on _ a _ ty-rant is sweet-est_ of_ all.

How sweet the answer

(*The Wren*)
original key

from Thomas Moore's *Irish Melodies*

Arranged by
BENJAMIN BRITTEN

Sail on, sail on*

(The Humming of the Ban)

original key

from Thomas Moore's *Irish Melodies*

Arranged by
BENJAMIN BRITTEN

Quietly rocking

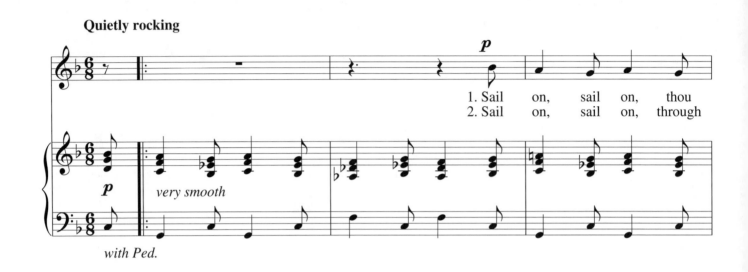

* *in original publication this song follows "Avenging and bright."*

The Minstrel Boy
(*The Moreen*)
original key

from Thomas Moore's *Irish Melodies*

Arranged by
BENJAMIN BRITTEN

At the mid hour of night

(*Molly, my Dear*)

original key

from Thomas Moore's *Irish Melodies*

Arranged by
BENJAMIN BRITTEN

Ech - o far off thro' the vale my sad o - ri - son rolls, I

think, oh my Love! 'tis thy voice from the king - dom of souls Faint - ly

an - swer - ing still the notes which once were so dear!

Ped. to the end

Rich and rare

(*The Summer is coming*)
original key

from Thomas Moore's *Irish Melodies*

Arranged by
BENJAMIN BRITTEN

Gently moving

Rich and rare were the gems she wore, And a bright gold ring on her wand she bore; But O her beau - ty was far be - yond Her spar - kling gems and her snow - white wand.

Dear Harp of my Country!

(*Kate Tyrrel*)
original key

from Thomas Moore's *Irish Melodies*

Arranged by
BENJAMIN BRITTEN

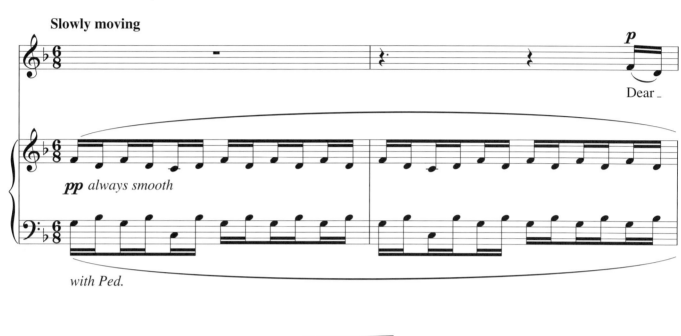

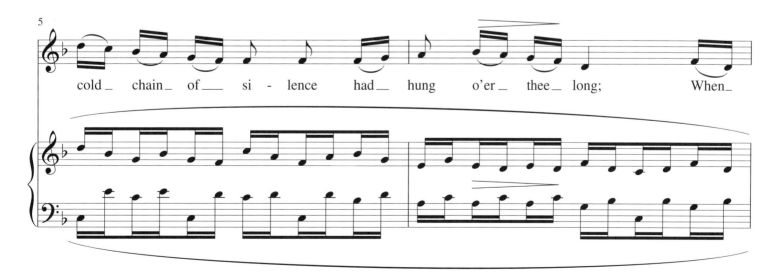

proud - ly, my own Is - land Harp! I un - bound thee, And __

gave __ all __ thy __ chords to light, __ free - dom, and song! The

warm lay of __ love and the light tone __ of glad - ness Have __

wak - en'd _ thy _ fond - est, _ thy _ live - li - est _ thrill; But so

oft hast thou ech - o'd the deep sigh of sad - ness, That _

e'en _ in _ thy _ mirth it will _ steal from thee still.

Dear _ Harp of my Coun - try! fare -

Oft in the stilly night

original key

from Thomas Moore's *Irish Melodies*

Arranged by
BENJAMIN BRITTEN

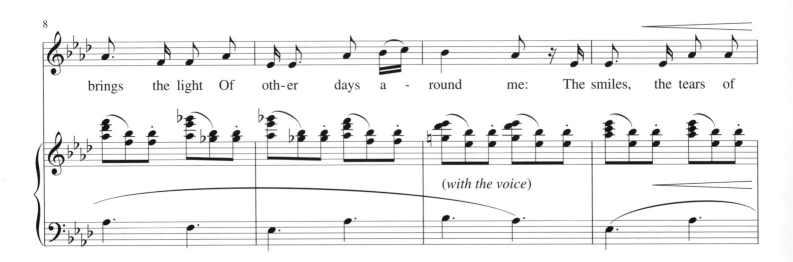

more sonorous

When I re-mem-ber all The friends, so link'd to-geth - er, _____ I've seen a-round me fall Like leaves in win-try __ weath - er, I feel like one Who treads a-lone Some ban-quet-hall de-sert - ed, Whose lights are fled, Whose

pp

sim.

gar - lands dead, And all but he de - part - ed!

Thus in the still - y night Ere slum - ber's chain has

bound___ me, Sad Mem - 'ry brings the light Of oth - er days a -

round me.___

The last rose of summer

(Groves of Blarney)
original key

from Thomas Moore's *Irish Melodies*

Arranged by
BENJAMIN BRITTEN

them; Thus kind-ly I scat-ter Thy leaves o'er the

bed Where thy mates of the

gar - den Lie sense - less and dead.

In time and moving forward

So soon may I fol-low, When friend - ships de -

O the sight entrancing

(*Planxty Sudley*)

original key

from Thomas Moore's *Irish Melodies*

Arranged by
BENJAMIN BRITTEN

Fast and brilliant

1. O the sight en-tranc - ing, When morn-ing's beam is glanc - ing O'er
2. Yet 'tis not helm or feath - er— For ask yon des-pot wheth - er His

files ar-ray'd With helm and blade, And plumes in the gay wind danc - ing. When
plum-éd bands Could bring such hands And hearts as ours to-geth - er. Leave

(without Ped.)

FOLKSONG ARRANGEMENTS
Volume 5
British Isles

The Brisk Young Widow

original key

*Words and Melody
collected by CECIL SHARP

Arranged by
BENJAMIN BRITTEN

Copyright in U.S.A. 1958 by Boosey & Co., Ltd.
© under U.C.C. 1961 by Boosey & Co., Ltd.

2. A
4. O

lov - er soon there came,   A brisk young farm - er,   With his hat turn'd up all
mad - am, don't be coy   For all your glo - ry,   For __ fear of an - oth - er

mf

(heavy)

round,   Seek - ing to gain her.   My __ dear, for love of you   This
day   And an - oth - er sto - ry.   If the world on you should frown   Your

wide world I'd go through   If __ you will but prove true   You shall wed a farm - er.
top - knot must come down   To a Lind - sey - wool - sey gown.   Where is then your glo - ry?

f

last there came that way A soot-y col-lier, With his hat bent down all

with Ped.

round, He soon did gain her: Where-at the farm-er swore; "The

wid-ow's mazed, I'm sure. I'll _ nev-er court no more A _ brisk young wid-ow!"

Sally in our Alley

original key

Words and Music by
HENRY CAREY

Arranged by
BENJAMIN BRITTEN

1. Of all the girls that are so smart There's none like Pret - ty
2. Of all the days with in the week, I dear - ly love but

Sal - ly; She is the dar - ling of my heart And lives in our
one day, And that's the day that comes be - tween A Sat - ur - day and

al - ley. There's ne'er a la - dy in the land That's half so sweet as
Mon - day, For then I'm dressed all in my best, To walk a - broad with

bangs me most se-vere-ly: But let him bang his bel-ly-ful I'll
soon as text is nam-ed; I leave the Church in ser-mon-time And

bear it all for Sal-ly; } She is the dar-ling of my heart And
slink a-way to Sal-ly; }

lives in our al-ley. al-ley.

5. My mas-ter

with Ped.

The Lincolnshire Poacher

original key

Arranged by
BENJAMIN BRITTEN

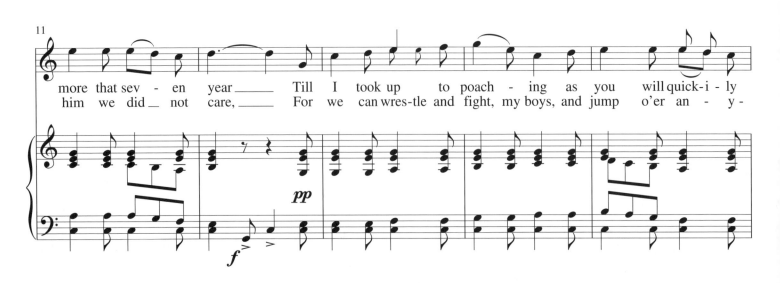

took the hare a-live, my boys, and thro' the woods did steer,
sold him for a crown, my boys, but I did not tell you where,
O 'tis

my de-light on a shin-ing night, in the sea-son of the year.

year. 5. Suc-

cess to ev-er-y gen-tle-man that lives in Lin-coln-shire, Suc-

Early one morning

original key

Arranged by
BENJAMIN BRITTEN

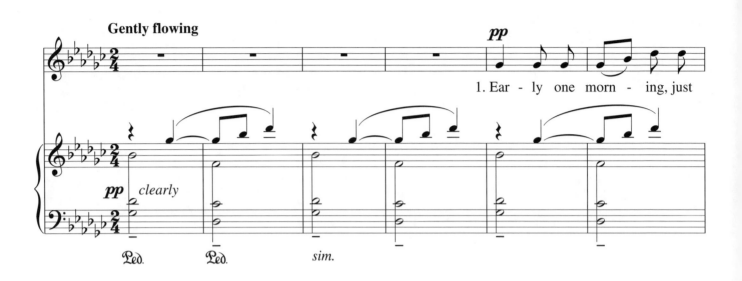

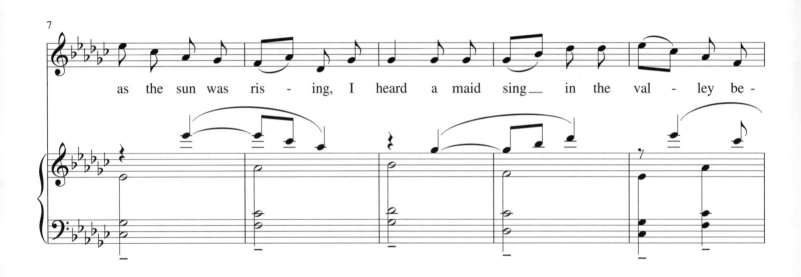

poor _ maid-en   so?   3. Re - mem - ber the   vows _ that you

made _ to your Ma - ry,   Re - mem - ber the   bow'r _ where you   vow'd _ to be   true;

O   don't de - ceive _ me,   O   nev - er   leave _ me!

How _ could you   use _   a _   poor _ maid-en   so?"

Ca' the yowes

original key

Words by
ROBERT BURNS

Arranged by
BENJAMIN BRITTEN

Then a - fold - ing let us gang, My bon - nie dea - rie.
O'er the waves that sweet - ly glide To the moon sae clear - ly.
I can die but can - na part, My bon - nie dea - rie.

1st and 2nd times | *last time*

cresc.

dim.

broadly
pp *freely*

Ca' the yowes to the knowes, Ca' them where the heath - er growes,

pp

ppp

Ca' them where the bur - nie rowes, My bon - nie dea - rie.

ppp

pppp

FOLKSONG ARRANGEMENTS
Volume 6
England

I will give my love an apple

original key

*Words and Melody from
"Folk Songs for Schools"
collected and arranged by
H. E. D. HAMMOND and R. VAUGHAN WILLIAMS

Folk Song from Dorset
Arranged for voice and guitar by
BENJAMIN BRITTEN
Transcribed for piano by
Richard Walters

Gently moving

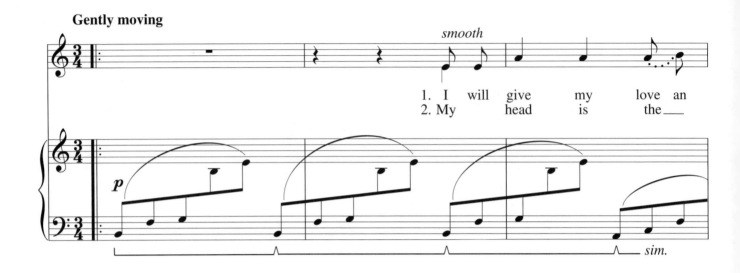

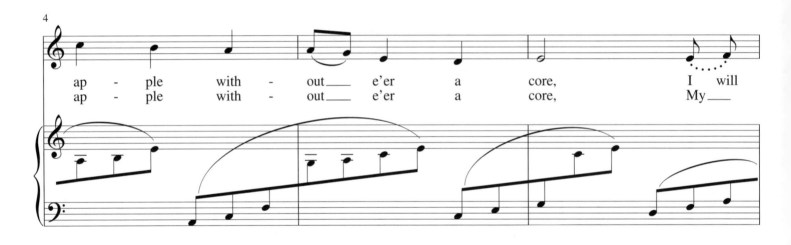

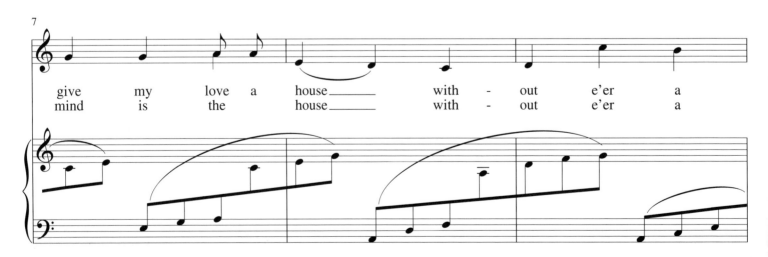

Sailor-boy
original key

*Words and Melody from
"Seventeen Nursery Songs from the
Appalachian Mountains" (under the title 'Soldier Boy')
collected and arranged by CECIL J. SHARP

Folk Song from the
Appalachian Mountains of Kentucky
Arranged for voice and guitar by
BENJAMIN BRITTEN
Transcribed for piano by
Richard Walters

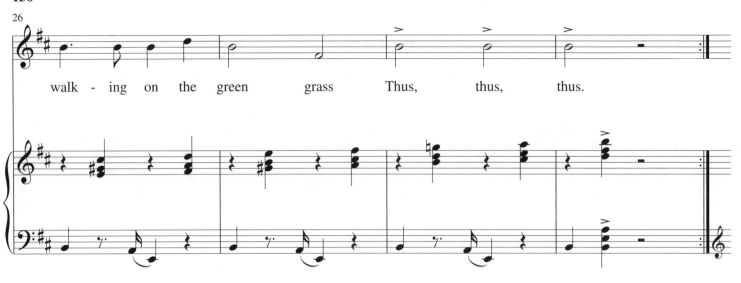

walk - ing on the green grass Thus, thus, thus.

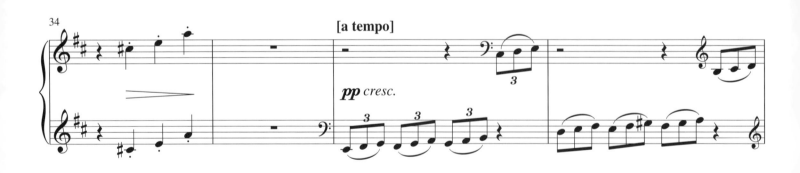

Master Kilby

original key

*Words and Melody from
"Folk Songs for Schools"
collected and arranged by CECIL J. SHARP

Folk Song from Somerset
Arranged for voice and guitar by
BENJAMIN BRITTEN
Transcribed for piano by
Richard Walters

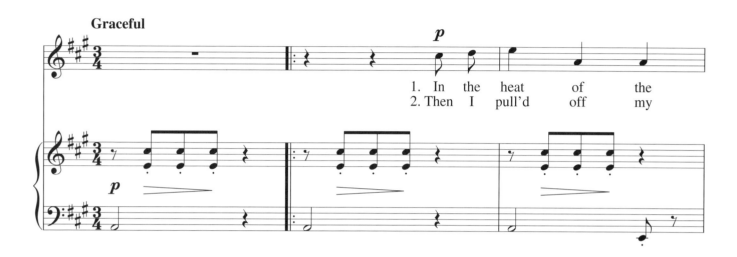

all for the sake of_____ my_ charm-ing Nan - cy.

6. She's the fair - est of girls, She's the

choice of my own_ heart, She is paint - ed like wax - work_____ In_

e - ve - ry part."_____

The Soldier and the Sailor

original key

*Collected by CECIL J. SHARP
in Oxfordshire, August 1909

Folk Song from Oxfordshire
Arranged for voice and guitar by
BENJAMIN BRITTEN
Transcribed for piano by
Richard Walters

Heavy and rhythmic (♩.)

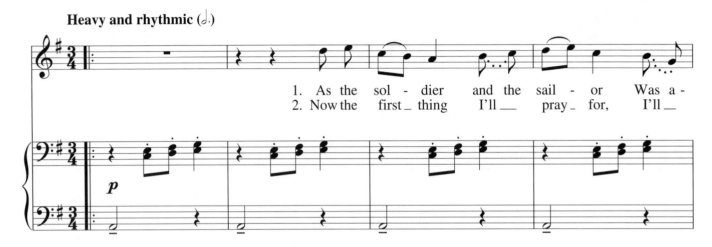

1. As the sol - dier and the sail - or Was a -
2. Now the first _ thing I'll _ pray _ for, I'll _

walk - ing one day, Said the sol - dier to the sail - or: __ I've a
pray _ for the Queen, That _ she have peace and plen - ty __ All the

mind __ for to pray. Pray _ on then, said the sail - or, Pray _
days __ of her reign, And _ where she got __ one man I __

one ship I___ wish she had___ ten; And___ nev-er want for a

Na - vy. Said the sail - or: A - men. 4. Now the

next___ thing I'll___ pray___ for, is a pot___ of good beer, For good

liq - uor were___ sent us___ our spir - its to___ cheer, And___

Bonny at Morn

original key

*Words and Melody from
"North Country Folk Songs"
by W. G. WHITTAKER

Folk Song from Northumberland
Arranged for voice and guitar by
BENJAMIN BRITTEN
Transcribed for piano by
Richard Walters

The Shooting of His Dear
original key

*Words and Melody from
"Six Folk Songs from Norfolk"
collected and arranged by E. J. MOERAN

Folk Song from Norfolk
Arranged for voice and guitar by
BENJAMIN BRITTEN
Transcribed for piano by
Richard Walters

37 shot_ my own true love in the room of a swan."

more agitated

42 Then out came bold un - cle with his locks hang - ing

46 grey, Say - ing, "Jim - my, dear Jim - my, don't you go__ a -

50 way Don't you leave_ your own coun - try till the

EIGHT FOLKSONG ARRANGEMENTS
(1976)

Lord! I married me a wife

original key: E minor

Arranged for voice and harp by
BENJAMIN BRITTEN
arranged for piano by
Colin Matthews

She's like the swallow

original key

Arranged for voice and harp by
BENJAMIN BRITTEN
arranged for piano by
Colin Matthews

flies so high, She's like the riv - er that nev - er runs dry, She's like the sun - shine on the lee shore, I

love my love ___ and love is no more.

Lemady
original key

Arranged for voice and harp by
BENJAMIN BRITTEN
arranged for piano by
Colin Matthews

flow-ers _____ that grows in yon - der green. O _____ yes I'll a-

rise _____ and pluck lil - ies, pinks and ros - es All

for my dear - est Le - ma - dy, the girl I a - dore.

O Le - ma - dy, O Le - ma - dy _____ what a

Bonny at Morn

original key

Arranged for voice and harp by
BENJAMIN BRITTEN
arranged for piano by
Colin Matthews

[Gently rocking]

pp smooth

cresc.

1. The   sheep's ___ in the mead - ows, The ___
2. The   bird's ___   in the nest, ___   The ___

mf

kye's ___   in the corn, ___   Thou's   o - wer   lang ___ in thy   bed,
trout's ___ in the burn, ___   Thou   hind - ers   thy ___ moth - er   In

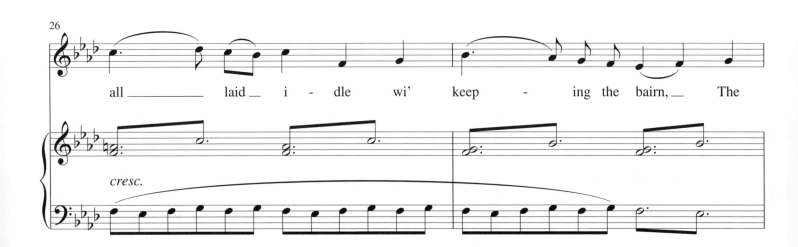

I was lonely and forlorn

(Bugeilio'r Gwenith Gwyn)

original key

Arranged for voice and harp by
BENJAMIN BRITTEN
arranged for piano by
Colin Matthews

While the seas do ebb and flow, and
Tra bo dwr y môr yn hallt, *A*

min - utes do not fal - ter; And while my heart beats
thra bo 'ngwallt yn ty - fu; *A thra bo cal - on*

in my breast, My 'flic - tion ne'er will _ al - ter. _
yn fy mron, Mi fydd - ai'n ffydd - lon _ i - ti. _

Ne'er shall I kiss her cheeks so fair, Nor feel her arms em-
Dy-wed i - mi'r gwir heb gêl, A rho dan sêl d'a-

brac - ing:___ For I had watched the ripe - ning wheat, Yet
teb - ion:___ P'run ai my - fi, ai ar - all, Gwen, Sydd

oth - ers reaped her lov - ing.___
or - au gen dy ga - lon?___

David of the White Rock

(*Dafydd y Garreg Wen*)
original key

Arranged for voice and harp by
BENJAMIN BRITTEN
arranged for piano by
Colin Matthews

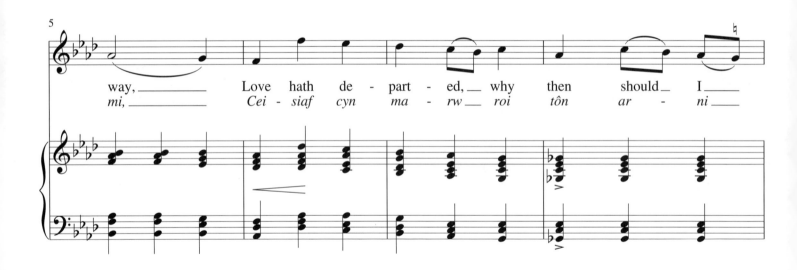

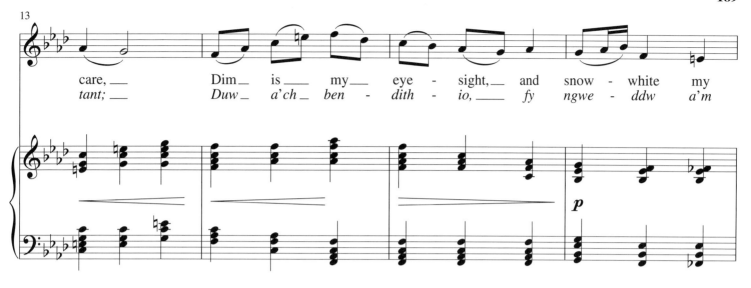

care, ___ Dim __ is __ my __ eye - sight, ___ and snow - white my
tant; ___ *Duw __ a'ch __ ben - dith - io, ___ fy ngwe - ddw a'm*

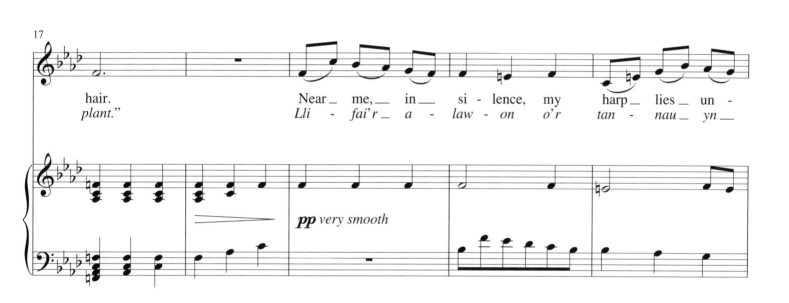

hair. Near __ me, __ in __ si - lence, my harp __ lies __ un -
plant." *Lli - fai'r __ a - law - on o'r tan - nau __ yn __*

strung, _____ Weak are my fin - gers, __ and falt - 'ring __ my __ tongue!
lli, _____ Me - lys oedd cein - ciau __ fy nhe - lyn __ i ___ mi.

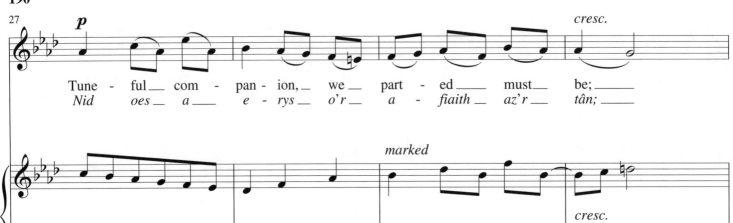

Tune - ful __ com - pan - ion, __ we __ part - ed __ must __ be; __
Nid oes a __ e - rys o'r a - fiaith __ az'r tân; __

Thou __ canst __ no __ long - er __ bring com - fort to me.
Gwyw - odd __ yr __ a - wen, a tha - wodd y gân.

Yet __ ere __ we sev - er, thy mas - ter __ would __ fain __ Swan - like ex -
"Nei - thiwr __ mi __ glyw - ais lais an - gel __ fel __ hyn: __ 'Da - fydd, tyrd

pire in ___ a last dy - ing ___ strain; And when a -
a - dref, _ a chan - a ___ trwy'r _ glyn.' De - lyn ___ fy ___

bove him __ the __ cy - press bough __ wave, __ Spir - its ___ shall __ mur - mur _ it
me - byd! _ ffar - wel i ___ dy ___ dant. __ Duw __ a'ch _ ben - dith - io, ___ fy

o - ver his grave.
ngwe - ddw a'm plant."

The False Knight upon the Road*

original key: F Major

Arranged for voice and harp by
BENJAMIN BRITTEN
arranged for piano by
Colin Matthews

* *No tempo is given in the original edition.*

© 1980 by Faber Music, Ltd.

Bird Scarer's Song

original key

Arranged for voice and harp by
BENJAMIN BRITTEN
arranged for piano by
Colin Matthews

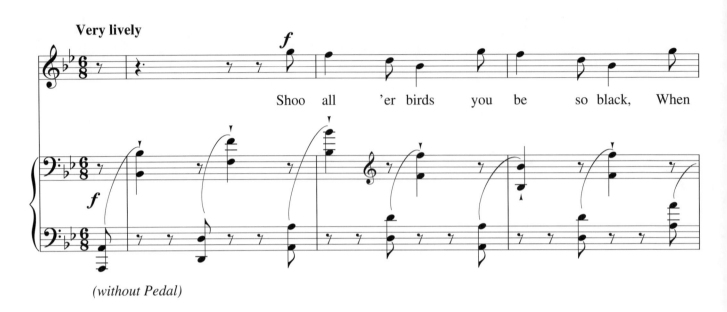

Start slow and soft, with accel. and cresc.

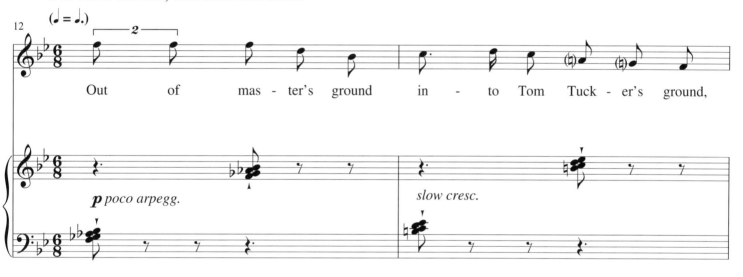

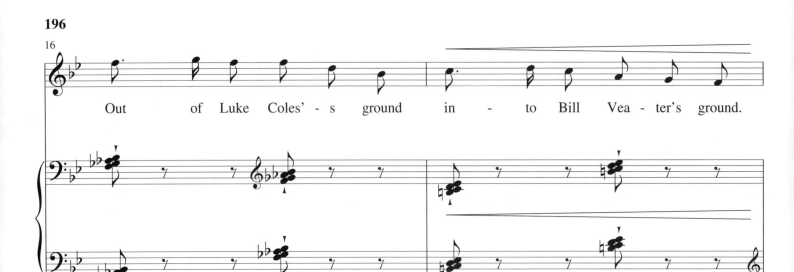

Out of Luke Coles'-s ground in - to Bill Vea - ter's ground.

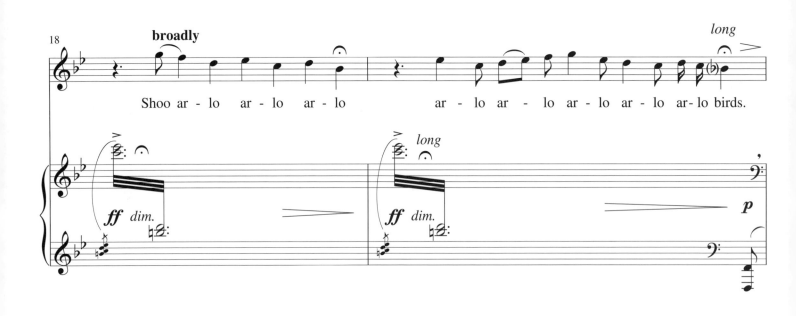

Shoo ar - lo ar - lo ar - lo ar - lo ar - lo ar - lo ar - lo ar- lo birds.

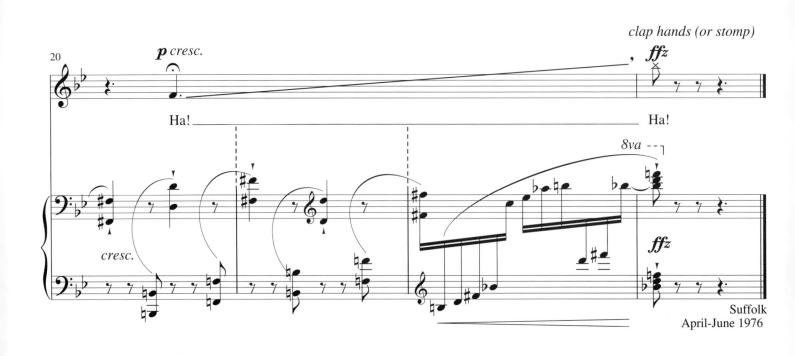

Ha! Ha!

Suffolk
April-June 1976

TOM BOWLING
AND OTHER SONG ARRANGEMENTS
(published 2001)

Tom Bowling
from The Oddities
original key

Words and music by
CHARLES DIBDIN (1745-1814)

Realized by
BENJAMIN BRITTEN

Slow march

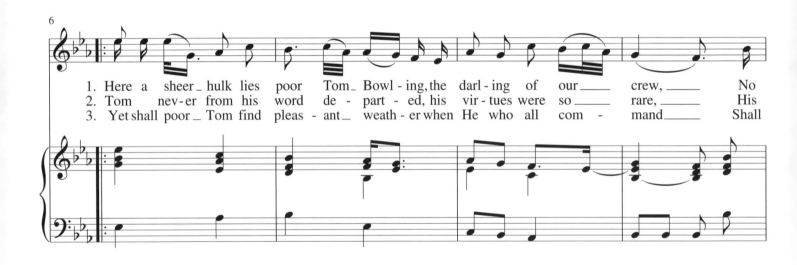

1. Here a sheer — hulk lies poor Tom — Bowl - ing, the darl - ing of our — crew, — No
2. Tom nev-er from his word de - part - ed, his vir - tues were so — rare, — His
3. Yet shall poor — Tom find pleas - ant — weath - er when He who all com - mand — Shall

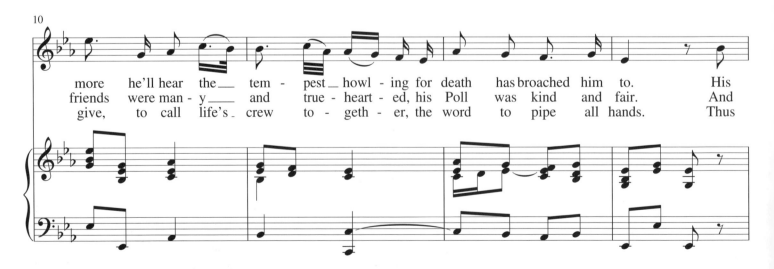

more he'll hear the — tem - pest howl - ing for death has broached him to. His
friends were man - y — and true - heart - ed, his Poll was kind and fair. And
give, to call life's — crew to - geth - er, the word to pipe all hands. Thus

form was of the man - liest beau - ty, his heart was kind_ and_ soft,_____
then he'd sing so blithe_ and jol - ly, ah, many's the time_ and_ oft,_____ But
Death, who kings and tars_ de - spatch - es, in vain Tom's life_ hath_ doff'd,_____ For

Faith - ful be - low Tom did_____ his du - ty, and now he's gone a - loft,_____ and
mirth_ is turned to mel - an - chol - y, for Tom is gone a - loft,_____ for
though_ his bod - y's un - der hatch - es, his soul is gone a - loft,_____ his

repeat for verses two and three

now_ he's gone_ a - loft.
Tom_ is_ gone_ a - loft.
soul_ is_ gone_ a - loft.

pp

(pp)

The Crocodile

from English County Songs
original key

Words and melody collected by
L. BROADWOOD and J. A. FULLER MAITLAND

Arranged by
BENJAMIN BRITTEN

Dink's Song

from American Ballads and Folk Songs

original key

Words and melody collected by
JOHN A. LOMAX and ALAN LOMAX

Arranged by
BENJAMIN BRITTEN

* Spelt 'Norah' in the text used as Britten's source.

Greensleeves

Traditional Folk Song

original key

Arranged by
BENJAMIN BRITTEN

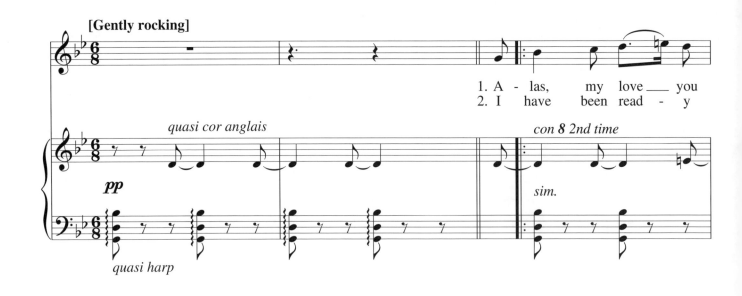

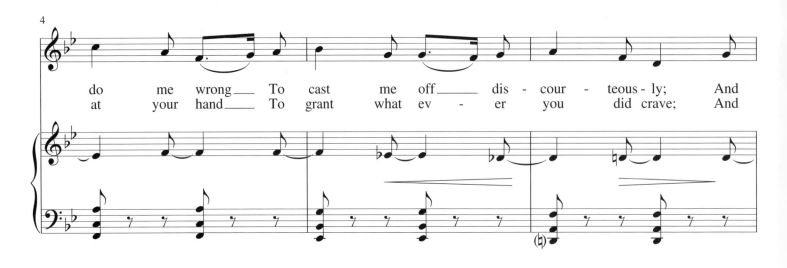

com - pa - ny. }
for to gain. }
Green - sleeves _ was all my joy, _____ Green - sleeves was

my de - light. Green - sleeves was my heart of gold, __ And who but my la - dy

Green - sleeves?

The Holly and the Ivy

Traditional Folk Song
original key

Words and melody collected by
CECIL SHARP

Arranged by
BENJAMIN BRITTEN

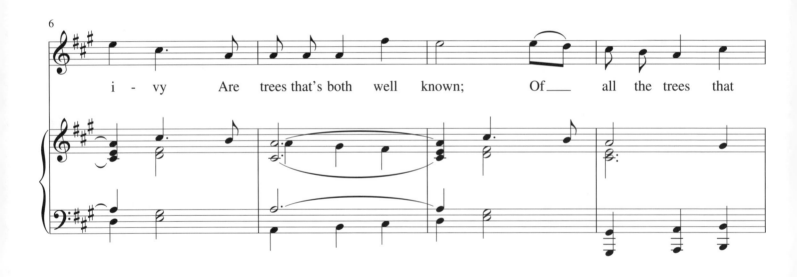

ris - ing of the sun, __ The run - ning of the deer, The __

play - ing of the mer - ry harp, Sweet __ sing - ing in the choir.

The hol - ly bears a blos - som, As white as an - y

flower; And __ Ma - ry bore sweet Je - sus Christ To __ be our sweet Sa -

I wonder as I wander

from Songs of the Hill Folk

original key

Words and melody collected by
JOHN JACOB NILES

Arranged by
BENJAMIN BRITTEN

under the sky How Je - sus our Sa - viour did come for to die For

poor or' - n'ry peo - ple like you and like I, I won - der as I wan - der out

un - der the sky._____ When

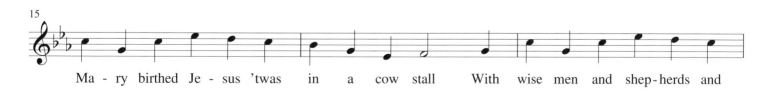

Ma - ry birthed Je - sus 'twas in a cow stall With wise men and shep - herds and

farm - ers and all, On high from God's heav - en the stars' light did fall And the

prom - ise of the a - ges it did then re - call. _____

poco animato

mf

poco f

If

pp

Je - sus had want - ed for an - y wee thing, A star in the sky or a

bird on the wing Or all of God's an - gels in Heav'n for to sing, He

animato

sure - ly could-'ve had it for he was the King! _____

f

I won - der as I wan - der out un - der the sky How

Je - sus our Sa - viour did come for to die For poor or' - n'ry peo - ple like

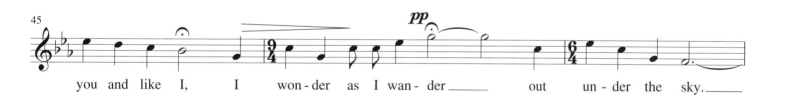

you and like I, I won - der as I wan - der_____ out un - der the sky._____

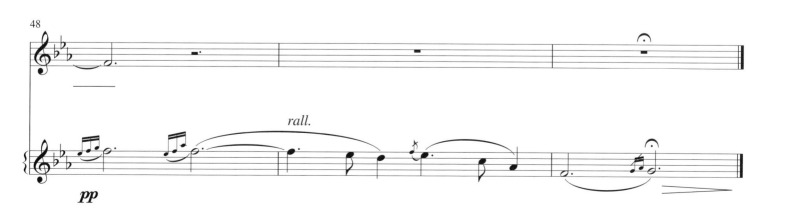

Pray goody
from Hullah's Song Book
original key

Words by KANE O'HARA
Melody by CHARLES BURNEY

Arranged by
BENJAMIN BRITTEN

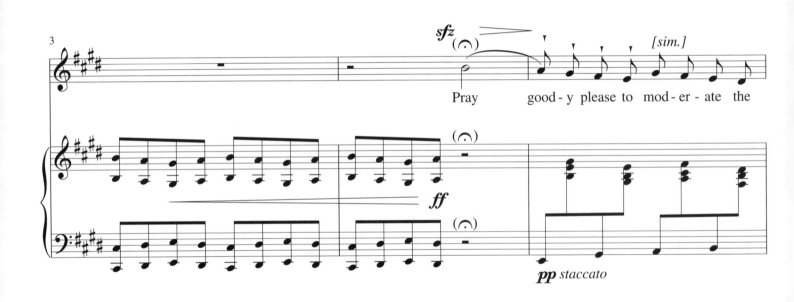

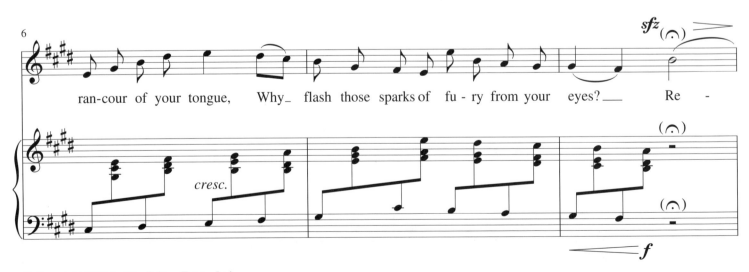

The Deaf Woman's Courtship

Appalachian Folk Song
original key: F Major

Words and melody collected by
CECIL SHARP

Arranged by
BENJAMIN BRITTEN

Soldier, won't you marry me?

Appalachian Folk Song

original key

Words and melody collected by
CECIL SHARP

Arranged by
BENJAMIN BRITTEN

'Sol - dier, sol - dier won't you mar - ry me? It's_ O a fife and drum.'

The Stream in the Valley

(Da unten im Tale)

original key

German Folk Song
English translation by IRIS ROGERS

Arranged by
BENJAMIN BRITTEN

* Throughout, play small sized piano notes only in the absence of a cello.

Lyrics:
You tell me you love me, You tell me you're true,__ But a lit - tle de - ceiv - ing Is sure - ly there too.

If I tell you a thou - sand times

That I am true___ And if still you won't heed me Then I'll go from

you.

The Stream in the Valley

(Da unten im Tale)
original key

Cello

German Folk Song
English translation by IRIS ROGERS

Arranged by
BENJAMIN BRITTEN

This part page can be carefully detached from the book.